MAZEL TOV Y'ALL

The Ultimate Southern–Jewish Bake Book

SARA KASDAN
Author of
LOVE and KNISHES

ALEXANDER Books™
Founded 332 B.C.
a division of Creativity, Inc.
65 Macedonia Road
Alexander, NC 28701 USA
(704) 255-8719

Publisher: Ralph Roberts

Vice President/Publishing: Pat Roberts

Cover Design: Brett Putnam

Editors: Barbara Blood, Susan Parker

Interior Design and Electronic Page Assembly: **WorldComm**®

Printed in the United States of America

10 9 8 7 6 5 4 3 2 1

Library of Congress Cataloging-in-Publication

Kasdan, Sara.
Mazel tov y'all : the ultimate southern-Jewish bake book / Sara Kasdan.
p. cm.
Reprint. Originally published: New York : Vanguard Press, 1968.
Includes index.
ISBN 1-57090-080-9 (alk. paper)
1. Baking. 2. Cookery, Jewish. I. Title.
TX765.K34 1998 98-2870
641.8'15--dc21 CIP

Alexander Books—a division of Creativity, Inc.–is a full-service publisher located at 65 Macedonia Road, Alexander NC 28701. Phone (828) 252-9515 or (828) 255-8719 fax. For orders only: 1-800-472-0438. Visa and MasterCard accepted.

Alexander Books are distributed to the trade by Midpoint Trade Books, Inc., 27 West 20th St., New York N.Y. 10011, (212) 727-0190, (212) 727-0195 fax.

Contents

1. Pardon My Chutzpah 11

2. You Have to Be an Expert 13

3. Bar Mitzvah Goodies that Make Pretty the Table 15

Bourbon Balls 15
Chocolate Cherries 16
Chocolate Rose Leaves 16
Frosted Grapes 17

4. Bar Mitzvah 19

5. Lekach (Honey Cake) For All 21

Honey Cake 21-22
Honey Cake with Brandy 22
Fruited Honey Cake 23
Honey Cake in a Roaster 24

6. We Don't Spend it All in One Place 25

7. The Bah-Mitzvy Baker, Bless Her! 29

8. Mitzvah Bars 33

Apricot Bars 34
Bachelor Bars 34
Apricot Bars 35
Cherry Coconut Bars 36
Chocolate De-lite Bars 36
Coconut Bars 37
Date Bars 38
Dream Bars 38-39
Mother's Dream Bars 39
Pecan Bars 40
Meringue Bars 40

9. The Etiquette of Bar-Mitzvah Baking 43

10. So You Should Know What a Cake Is! 47

Apple Cake 47
Chiffon Cake for Shabbos 48
Chocolate Fruit Torte 49
Torte Frosting 49
Chocolate Layer Cake 50
Quick Mocha Icing 50
Ann Bush's Sour Cream Icing 51
My Friend Bessie's Cream-Cheese Icing 51
Danish Gold Cake 51

Date Cake ... 52
Date Cake Glaze ... 52
Favorite Fruit Torte ... 53
Feather Cake ... 53
Fruit Cocktail Cake ... 54
Ginger Cake ... 54
Grandmother's Black Coffee Cake ... 55
Hickory Nut Cake ... 55
White Mountain Cream ... 56
Kentucky Pecan Cake ... 57
Maple Nut Cake ... 58
Maple Nut Cake Icing ... 58
Meringue Spice Cake ... 58
Mock Pound Cake ... 59
Orange Cake ... 59
Orange Icing ... 60
Orange Delight Cake ... 60
Orange Delight Frosting ... 61
Pauline Cook's Cake ... 61
Pineapple Fluff Cake ... 62
My Best Pound Cake ... 62
Pound Cake ... 63
Prune Cake ... 64
Prune Cake Icing ... 64
Prunella Cake ... 64
Uncooked Frosting ... 65
Pumpkin Cake ... 65
Caramel Icing ... 65
Raisin Cake ... 66
Royale Chocolate Torte ... 66
Red Velvet Cake ... 67
Texas Pecan Pound Cake ... 68
Aunt Dora's Tomato Soup Cake ... 69
Whipped Cream Cake ... 69
White Cake ... 70
Seven-Minute Frosting ... 70

11. There's Nothing Like a Bar Mitzvah 71

Challah (Sabbath Twist Loaf) ... 72
Eier Kichlech ... 75
Eier Kichel ... 76
Kichel ... 77

12. An Engagement is a Happy Occasion No Matter What 79

Almond Horns ... 82
Cherry Thumb Prints ... 82
Chocolate Thumb Prints ... 83
Cinnamon Nut Crisps ... 84
Delcas ... 84
French Pastry Crescents ... 85
Fruit Slices ... 86
German Sour Cream Twists ... 86
Hard-Boiled Egg Cookies ... 87

Hungarian Butter Wreaths 88
Kipfel 89
Ruggelach (Yeast Horns) 90
Southern Pecan Tartlets 91
Sugar Cookies 92
Tiny Schnecken and Tartlets 92
Twist Craze—1964 93
Viennese Wafers 94

13. Grandchildren are Always a Happy Occasion **95**

Brownies 97
Chocolate Peanut Clusters 97
Cooky Rings 98
Doughnuts 99
Sugar Cookies 99

14. *A* is a Happy Occasion **101**

Banana Nut Loaf 103
Chocolate Cake 104
Chocolate Frosting 104
Chocolate Sponge Cake 104
Chocolate Cake With Yeast 105
Quick Chocolate Cake 106
Date-Nut Loaf 106
Hot Milk Cake 107
Crumb Frosting 107

15. C is for Carrot Cake **109**

Mama's Carrot Cake 111
Carrot Cake 112
Carrot Cake Glaze/Frosting 112

16. Happy Birthday to You **113**

Cream Cheese Cake With Walnut Crust 115
Cream Cheese Pie with Cointreau 116
Helen Saul's Cheese Cake 117
Strawberry Glaze 117
Cheese Torte 118
Chocolate Chip Cheese Cake 118
No Crust Cream Cheese Pie 119
Party Cheese Cake 120

17. Be It Never So Humble **121**

18. Coffee Cakes and Sweet Rolls that Make Lifelong Friends **125**

Babka (Yeast Coffee Cake) 125
Basic Sweet Yeast Dough 126
Coffee Cake Filling 126
Becie's Coffee Cake 127
Blueberry Coffee Cake 128
Coffee Cake 128
Coffee-Break Cake 130
Coffee Cake Supreme 131

Cottage Cheese Sweet Rolls 132
Cream Cheese Coffee Cake 132
Crumb-Filled Coffee Cake 132
Form Coffee Cake 134
Confectioners Icing 134
French Coffee Cake 135
French Coffee Cake 136
Mama Annie's Coffee Cake 136
Meringue Coffee Cake 137
Pull-Apart Coffee Cake 138
Sour Cream Coffee Cake 139
Streusel Coffee Cake 139
Mother's Viennese Kugelhof 140
Pinwheel Rolls 141
Schnecken 142
Viennese Schnecken 143
Viennese Schnecken for Muffin Tins 143

19. Strudel and other Traditional Meicholim 145

Bessie's Strudel 150
Cottage Cheese Strudel 151
Strudel à la Sadie 152
Ice Cream Strudel 153
Cream Cheese Strudel 154
Cheese Dreams 154
Hamentaschen 155
Poppy Seed Filling 156
Prune Filling 156
Cheese Hamentaschen 156
Cheese Filling 157
Hamentaschen 157
Prune Filling 157
Cheese Filling 158
Mandel Brodt 158-59
Mandel Bread 159
Periskes 160
Aunt Annie Kasdan's Tayglech 161
Aunt Ida's Party Tayglech 162
Quick Tayglech 163

20. Pesach isn't Pesach anymore 165

Passover Almond-Carrot Cake 168
Passover Apple Squares 169
Passover Apricot Whipped Pie 169
Passover Brownies 170
Bessie's Passover Chiffon Cake 170
Passover Cheese Cake 171
Passover Chocolate Cake 171
Chocolate Apple Torte 172
Passover Cookies 172
Date Torte 173
Passover Doughnuts 173

21. The Last Chapter 175

22. Index 185

Dedicated to Debbie, Vicki, and Harriet
May they have many happy occasions

ACKNOWLEDGMENT

I wish to thank the wonderful cooks who shared their prized recipes with me. Their names are listed at the end of the Index, beginning on page 177.

S.K.

Foreword

Such a good book this is!

Such *chutzpah* I have to even say that; gentile that I am, yet surrounded by mounds of steaming, delicious Jewish baked goods. *Ymmmmm*! So good! So good.

A *gentile*, of course, is a non-Jewish person and while I have been, so to speak, circumscribed in many places, I am not of the faith Judaic. *Chutzpah* is... well, there exist many definitions. The wonderful Sara Kasdan—who not only is Jewish but has introduced me to such exquisite delectations as *knishes* (for that alone, may she be blessed forever and a day!)—has her own definition of *chutzpah*. Hers you'll see in the following pages.

Mine? Well *chutzpah* is a *goy* like *moi* not only publishing a Jewish cookbook, but then *doing it again*, for the second time, yet!

He even eats bagels for breakfast. Such... well... such *chutzpah*.

Oy!

The truth is, someone *had* to do it. They just had to! Sara's work is timeless; the very epitomy of both Jewish humor and cooking, and every morsel totally delicious!

Sara Kasdan's first book—***Love and Knishes***—was published in 1956 by Vanguard in New York. It was kept in print for over 33 years, becoming the much beloved ultimate Jewish cookbook. A mouthwatering source for Jewish food both of the haute and not so haute cruisine. Then—as these things have a way of happening—Vanguard was bought out by another company and ***Love and Knishes*** dropped from print.

Came then *moi* the *goy* and Alexander Books.

The first time I spoke with Sara, I said to myself "such a nice lady this is... such a wonderful book she has!... but what are *knishes*?"

Knishes I found out about, and ate and ate! (You can find out, too, just call us at 1-800-472-0438 and order ***Love and Knishes***, the ultimate Jewish cookbook). We are now in our third printing; or more likely the fourth or fifth by the time you read this. We intend to keep it in print far longer than Vanguard's 33 years! (We are already over four years.)

"I have," Sara says to me one day, "a second book."

"Oh?" I ask, "and what is it's title?"

"It is," says she, ***"Mazel Tov Y'all, A Bake Book for Happy Occasions."***

"I will print it," is my instant reply.

This decision was a no brainer for me, being both a Southern by birth and choice, and (thanks to Sara) a now firm aficionado of Jewish food.

Mazel tov, by the way, is an old Yiddish term from the Hebrew meaning "good luck" or "congratulations." *Y'all* is from Southern American and means "you all" as in "*y'all* are purely gonna love this heah book."

So we now present to you our second book of Jewish food: ***Mazel Tov Y'all, the Ultimate Southern Jewish Bake Book.***

This stuff, I can tell you, is *sooo goooood*!

And if that's *chutzpah*, just consider this your second helping and enjoy! Enjoy!

—Ralph Roberts
Alexander, North Carolina
December 5, 1997

1

Pardon My Chutzpah

A number of years ago, I had the *chutzpah* to write a Jewish cookbook. Why do I say *chutzpah*? What made me think I could tell you how to cook Jewish dishes? Was I born knowing how to cook these delicacies? Did I learn from my mother? The answer is no but also yes. No, I didn't learn to cook them, but yes, I learned how to eat them. I learned how they should taste, so that when the time came that I wanted to learn how to cook, the memory of the taste, the flavor, the aroma stayed with me. I gathered recipes; I tested them. When they tasted like my memories I put them into a book which I called *Love and Knishes*.

While I was collecting recipes, I was also gathering stories, memories that were stilted up with every dish. In this way I learned that Jewish cooking is much more than just a collection of recipes.

The culture of a people is expressed through its eating habits. Many books have been written on this subject, but you don't have to read the books to recognize cultural differences. All you have to do is eat the food. This way you are learning and enjoying at the same time.

When you eat Italian food you realize that the Italians are a warm-blooded people given to earthy pleasures. The French are more sophisticated; to a Frenchman the sauce is most important. What started out as sauce for the goose (and also for the gander) has become a way of life.

German cooking is quite different from French and Italian. When you eat German food you know that the

Germans are a solid, substantial folk, no nonsense about them.

And what about Jewish cooking? Well, when you eat Jewish cooking you realize that for more than four thousand years, the Jewish people have suffered! And through their suffering they have learned that nothing lifts the spirits like a full stomach . . . you shouldn't be able to get up from the table to suffer.

What is Jewish cooking? For that matter, what are Jews? Do you think they are all alike? Never! Wherever Jews have lived (and where haven't they lived?) they've taken on protective coloration, and their habits and their speech differ from Jews of other countries. For example, the Russian Jews eat *ayer*, the Polish Jews eat *eier*, while the American Jews eat eggs. My husband is a Litvak. He doesn't eat any of these things. He eats a*pfeinkochen*—that's an omelet suffering from depression.

What is Jewish cooking? That's a difficult question. You say *kreplach* are Jewish? Yes, but if you are Italian you call them *ravioli*; if you are Chinese (and even if you aren't) you call them *won ton*. You think borsch is Jewish? It's Russian. Take the meat that is rolled in cabbage leaves, called *praakes*, *galuptzi* or *gevickelte kraut*, depending upon where your ancestors came from; if you are Armenian or Lebanese, you will wrap the meat in grape leaves. *Blintzes* are Jewish? Yes, but the Russians call them *blini*, the French call them *crêpes*.

Now you'll ask me if there is such a thing as a truly Jewish dish? To tell the truth, I'm not really a scholar so I can't say for sure, but I believe that *tzimmes* is really Jewish. Why? What other people would have the imagination and the courage to put together such a combination of foods?

So if Jewish cooking is not Jewish cooking, why did I write a Jewish cookbook and why am I writing a Jewish bake book? You'll finish the book, then you'll know. You'll know that if it looks good, if it smells tantalizing, if it tastes delectable—it's Jewish cooking. But, I'm getting ahead of my story. I don't want to give away the happy ending!

❤ 2 ❤

You Have to Be an Expert

I have a friend Bessie (may she live to one hundred and twenty years and may I have the strength to endure her) who is always bothering me about one thing or another. Before I wrote *Love and Knishes* it wasn't so bad, but now that I'm a writer she won't let me alone. She can't stand it that women ask me for advice—how to cook this or that, how to prepare for a wedding or bar mitzvah.

"It isn't enough that you're a writer," says my friend Bessie. "Now you have to be an expert, too. Why should you think you know how to make bar mitzvahs?"

My answer to her is, "Why not?"

What's so difficult about it, can you tell me? Of course, there are some women who make everything seem difficult. They get so excited preparing for a bar mitzvah that they forget the most important essential, which is that for every bar mitzvah you must have a son thirteen years old. This happened to me. All my friends were having bar mitzvahs. I got so excited that I baked two thousand pieces of strudel before I remembered that I have three daughters, but no sons.

You know how it is: when you get the reputation for being an expert, you are forced to live up to it, so that eventually you become the expert that everyone thought you were. So here I am, a bar mitzvah expert who never prepared a bar mitzvah! This is as it should be. Who are the experts on child care—the mothers and fathers of large families? No, they don't have time for it. The true experts are the bachelor uncle, the old-maid aunt, or the mother-in-law whose mistake you married.

So who should be the bar mitzvah expert, the mother of six sons? No. She doesn't have the time for it. As soon as she has finished with one bar mitzvah, she has to go off for a rest cure. Her doctor says to her, "Forget about bar mitzvahs. If you don't you'll have the next one here in the sanitarium."

Since the mother doesn't want to break with tradition for such a traditional event, she forgets about it until the next one is almost upon her. Now she gets really nervous. She berates herself for having wasted so much time keeping house, cooking for the family, going to P.T.A., Hadassah, Sisterhood, and Council meetings. Also—and this is what weighs on her conscience the most—she went to a Mah-Jongg game once a week! Our mother doesn't know it, but it is the Mahj game that will save her.

No, the mother of six sons is too busy and nervous to be an expert. To be an expert requires calm and detachment. That is why I am the expert. It is easy to be calm and detached when your expertmanship will never be put to the test. The worst that can happen is that I'll have to eat my words, and since I've put all my words into recipes for bar mitzvah goodies, it's the best thing that could happen to anyone.

❤ 3 ❤

Bar Mitzvah Goodies that Make Pretty the Table

You'll get a kick out of this recipe from Sarah Trivers of Chattanooga, Tenn.

BOURBON BALLS

2 Tbs. cocoa
1 c. confectioners sugar
¼ c. bourbon (or rum)
2 Tbs. light corn syrup
2 c. vanilla-wafer crumbs
1 c. finely chopped nuts

Sift together cocoa and confectioners sugar. Stir in bourbon, which has been combined with corn syrup. Add vanilla-wafer crumbs and nuts. Mix well. Form into small balls.

Dust with confectioners sugar. Allow to dry. Store in tightly covered tin or freeze until ready to serve.

✡ ✡ ✡

Mrs. James A. (Naomi) Altman is accustomed to hearing guests at Louisville bar mitzvahs *ooh* and *aah* over her Chocolate Cherries. They're wonderful for prettying-up a cooky tray.

CHOCOLATE CHERRIES

8 oz. jar stemmed maraschino cherries
½ c. semi-sweet chocolate bits
2 Tbs. milk
2 oz. pecan chips*

Drain cherries well on paper toweling. Using an individual egg poacher, melt chocolate in milk, stirring until melted and well blended. (Chocolate must be of the right consistency to adhere to the cherries, but not so thick as to lose the shape of the fruit.)

Holding the cherry by the stem, dip the bottom half into the chocolate and then immediately into the pecan chips. Place on wax paper to cool. After finishing the entire process, place cherries in the freezer to set the coating. The cherries may be kept frozen until used.

*or finely chopped pecans

Ann Bush of Louisville, Kentucky makes a tray trimmer that's pretty enough to eat!

CHOCOLATE ROSE LEAVES

Real rose leaves, if available; if not, use ivy, philodendron or other smooth, sturdy leaves
1 pkg. semi-sweet chocolate bits
A water-color brush

Wash leaves. Dry thoroughly. Melt chocolate over hot water. Stir until smooth. Using a new water-color brush, paint underside of leaves with a smooth, thick coat of chocolate, spreading chocolate *just to edge.*

Refrigerate until chocolate is set and firm. Insert point of a paring knife at tip of leaf and peel real leaf from chocolate one. Quickly and gently place chocolate leaves on wax paper. Chill until ready to use.

"I like to set a beautiful table," says Julia Karg of Neosho, Missouri, "but I don't like waste. A penny saved is a penny earned. Frosted grapes solve my problem. I can have my centerpiece and eat it too."

FROSTED GRAPES

Grapes
2 egg whites
1 tsp. water
Finely granulated sugar

Wash grapes and dry well on paper towels. Break into small bunches.

In a small mixing bowl, slightly beat 2 egg whites with 1 teaspoon water. Put sugar into another small mixing bowl.

Dip a small bunch of grapes into egg whites and then into sugar, turning to coat grapes well. Allow grapes to dry on paper towels. Refrigerate until ready to use.

4

Bar Mitzvah

When an Orthodox Jewish boy arrives at the age of thirteen, he becomes a "son of the Commandment," a bar mitzvah. The ceremony of bar mitzvah takes place in the synagogue, where the boy is called up to the Torah to read the portion for the day. He will also recite a carefully memorized speech and receive a special blessing from the rabbi.

Having become bar mitzvah, the boy is considered, ritually, at least, to be an adult, accountable for his own deeds and misdeeds, and ready to assume his responsibilities as a member of the Jewish community.

In the old days of the *shtetl*, the Jewish village community of eastern Europe, the ritual of bar mitzvah was usually accompanied by a simple reception. The more pious the family, the more simple the reception. The refreshments usually consisted of a glass of *bramvin* (brandy) and *lekach* (honey cake) for all.

5

Lekach (Honey Cake) For All

Mrs. S. W. (Goldye) Spain of Houston, Texas, contributes this recipe from the files of her mother, Mrs. H. L. Hollander.

HONEY CAKE

1 c. oil
1 c. sugar
4 eggs
1¼ c. honey
6 c. sifted flour
2 tsp. baking soda
2 tsp. baking powder
1 tsp. cinnamon
1 c. cold coffee
Grated rind of 1 lemon
Grated rind of 1 orange
1 Tbs. vanilla extract
1 c. chopped dates
½ c. chopped pecans
½ c. raisins (optional)

Combine and beat until thoroughly blended 1 cup oil and 1 cup sugar. Add eggs, one at a time, beating after each addition. Add honey, mixing well.

Sift together flour, baking soda, baking powder and cinnamon. Add alternately with coffee to the first mixture.

Fold in remaining ingredients. Pour into two greased 10-inch tube pans or two 9¼-by-5¼-by-2¾ loaf pans. Bake at 325° until cake tests done, about 1 hour. Cool on racks. Turn out and serve unfrosted.

Mrs. I. M. Ziess of New Harmony, Indiana, bakes Honey Cakes as Rosh Hashonah gifts for her friends.

HONEY CAKE

5 eggs, separated
2 c. dark brown sugar
1 c. honey
½ c. strong black coffee
3 c. flour
1 tsp. baking soda
½ tsp. ground cloves
½ tsp. ground allspice
½ tsp. ground ginger
½ tsp. ground cinnamon

Beat egg yolks until thick. Blend in sugar, honey and coffee. Sift together flour, soda and spices. Fold into the first mixture. Stir until blended.

Fold in stiffly beaten egg whites.

Pour into a 9-by-9 pan which has been greased and lined with wax paper. Bake at 350° until it tests done, about 50-60 minutes.

A honey of a cake is the following from Mrs. Maurice Kline of Canton, Ohio:

HONEY CAKE WITH BRANDY

3 eggs
1 c. brown sugar
1 c. honey
¾ c. apple butter
4 c. sifted flour
2 tsp. baking powder
1 tsp. baking soda
1 tsp. cinnamon
1 tsp. nutmeg
1 tsp. ground allspice
1 tsp. ground ginger
½ tsp. salt
¾ c. strong coffee
3 Tbs. oil
1 tsp. vanilla extract
3 Tbs. cherry brandy
½ c. raisins
½ c. chopped nuts

Beat eggs and sugar thoroughly. Add honey and apple butter and beat again. Sift together all dry ingredients and add alternately with coffee to the first mixture. Blend in oil, vanilla and brandy. Fold in raisins and nuts. Pour into greased and wax-paper lined 10-inch tube pans. Bake at 350° until cake tests done, about 50-60 minutes.

Lois (Mrs. David) Rosenfield of Warwick, Rhode Island, loves reading cookbooks and trying out new recipes. Her Honey Cake, however, is from an old, time-tested recipe.

FRUITED HONEY CAKE

4 eggs
1 c. sugar
1 c. honey
2 Tbs. oil
½ c. strong coffee or tea
½ c. raisins
¼ c. mixed candied fruits or citron
½ c. chopped nuts
½ tsp. ground allspice
1 tsp. ground cloves
½ tsp. cinnamon
2 tsp. apricot or plum brandy (amount of brandy may be tripled if you're in the mood)
3⅔ c. flour
1½ tsp. baking powder
1 tsp. baking soda
Blanched almond halves

Beat eggs well. Add sugar gradually and continue beating until light.

Stir in honey, oil, coffee, fruits, nuts, spices and brandy. Stir together flour, baking powder and baking soda. Fold into first mixture.

Bake in an oiled and paper-lined 10-inch tube pan. Sprinkle a few almond halves on top. Bake at 310° for 1 hour. Invert to cool.

"I got this recipe from Mama," says Edith (Mrs. George) Alper of Wilmington, North Carolina. "As with all the recipes she gave me, Mama invariably left out at least one ingredient. After inspecting the finished product with a jaundiced eye, she would say, '*Vos fehlt*?' (What's missing?) 'The color is wrong, did you put in the coffee?' 'You didn't tell me coffee,' I would say. It was this way all down the line with the orange juice, oil, or spices. It took about five attempts before I finally baked the cake to suit Mama. It's a wonderful cake to bake for bar mitzvahs or *Oneg Shabbats* because it will serve sixty, not counting the ends that you can *nosh* in the kitchen."

HONEY CAKE IN A ROASTER

6 eggs
2 c. sugar, scant
2 c. honey
1 can (6 oz.) concentrated frozen orange juice
1 c. strong coffee
¼ c. oil
6½ c. flour
1 tsp. baking soda
2 tsp. baking powder
1 tsp. ground allspice

Beat eggs until light. Add sugar. Add honey. Continue beating until sugar is well dissolved. Add orange juice, coffee and oil. Continue beating for an additional minute or two.

Sift together flour, baking soda, baking powder and allspice.

Slowly fold into batter by hand. Beat, by hand, an additional minute or two.

Pour into a roasting pan, 10-by-15½-by-2, which has been greased and lined with wax paper. Top batter decoratively with whole almonds.

Bake at 350° for 30 minutes. Reduce heat to 325° and continue baking until cake tests done, about 45 more minutes.

6

We Don't Spend It All in One Place

Life was simple in the days of the *shtetl,* and bar mitzvahs were simple, but the world does not stand still. Styles change, even bar-mitzvah styles. Nowadays, a woman must begin preparing for a son's bar mitzvah even before she gets married. In the first place, she must choose a husband who will be a good provider . . . and not just brandy and cakes.

Today, the simple bar-mitzvah reception has turned into a buffet luncheon for five hundred people, not counting the children (actually, the children should be counted twice). This is only in the South and Midwest; in the East it's a dinner dance in a hall or hotel at $30 a plate minimum.

In the South and Midwest, it probably cost $30 a plate minimum, too, but we don't spend it all in one place. There's the sit-down dinner the night before for out-of-town guests, the reception (buffet luncheon) in the synagogue, the open house at home or at "the club," and the party for the young people.

About the New York catered affairs there's no point in writing. On catered affairs I'm no expert, and who needs experts? All you have to do is remember how Cousin

Sophie made hers, and you make yours better. She'll eat her heart out.

All you have to do for a catered affair is make up your mind either this hall or that hotel, either this orchestra or that one, either chicken or beef or both, either you invite all the relatives or just the ones you're talking to, either you invite all your friends or just the ones who will invite you back, either it costs more or it costs less.

Your husband thinks it should cost less; you think it should cost more. This is not a problem for me; it's a problem for a marriage counselor. It isn't even a problem for a marriage counselor, because you know that the more your husband spends for a bar mitzvah, the more he will have to brag about later. What is there to say about a $15-a-plate affair, if, indeed, there is one that cheap? You couldn't even mention the price without apologizing. You can talk about a $30-a-plate bar mitzvah even before it happens. As a matter of fact, you are honor-bound to do so. In the first place, the more expensive the bar mitzvah, the more flattered your guests will feel. Their status is automatically raised along with your own. In the second place, if you didn't let people know the cost of the affair how would they know what kind of gift to send? If they sent a $10 gift for a $30 bar mitzvah, they would feel cheap. You wouldn't want that to happen.

Another reason why your husband will agree to a more costly bar mitzvah is that he can't afford a cheap one. For business reasons alone, he can't afford it. People will think his business is failing, and creditors will start pressing for payment. The only people who can afford cheap bar mitzvahs are the ones who can afford the most expensive kind, including a trip to Israel for the whole family.

No, for an Eastern-type bar mitzvah you don't need me at all, but read me anyway, because I've got recipes here which from the reading alone you'll gain weight. If you don't need these recipes for a bar mitzvah, maybe you'll need them for an engagement, a wedding or even a Mah-jongg game. Maybe you'll read me just to give your stomach pleasure while you're dieting. Also, y'all'll learn how we make a "bah mitzvy" in the South, and how we have developed a new type of woman, the "bah-mitzvy baker," bless her!

❤ 7 ❤

The Bah-Mitzvy Baker, Bless Her!

I don't know why women make such a *tzimmes* out of preparing for a bar mitzvah. In the old days, before the invention of the freezer, it was a lot of trouble—everything had to be prepared at the last minute. But now, a mother can start baking bar-mitzvah cookies the day she brings her new son home from the hospital.

My friend Bessie has had a freezer since the first day they were put on sale. Bessie tells me that in all that time she has never been able to put her own food in her freezer. Someone is always saying to her, "Save my life. Let me put my bar mitzvah in your freezer." How can she refuse? After all, to help with a bar mitzvah is a *mitzvah,* the fulfillment of a Commandment.

When my friend Bessie bought her freezer, whatever it cost, it was a bargain. With it she has filled her quota of mitzvahs and earned her passage to heaven. She has had as many as five bar mitzvahs in her freezer at one time. One of the women who borrowed freezer space even had the *chutzpah* to say to Bessie, "Don't you think you need a bigger box? We could sell you one at a discount."

Personally, I think Bessie has done enough. Not only does she freeze for every bar mitzvah; she bakes, too! So I said to her one day, "Personally, Bessie, I think you've done enough. You haven't got an inch of space left. Your friends will understand if you ask them to take their stuff out and borrow another freezer."

"I couldn't do that," said Bessie, "it would be a sin."

"The trouble with you, Bessie, is you got a complex. The worst kind – a guilt complex! Must be you're feeling guilty, otherwise you wouldn't be such a *schmo*. You'd leave a little room in your freezer for emergencies."

Do you think she listened to me? I had to rent a commercial food locker for my daughter's wedding!

Take my word for it, freezers couldn't be more wonderful if they were invented specially for bar mitzvahs, but as wonderful as they are, there is an even greater invention – the bar-mitzvah bakers or, as we call them in the South, the bah-mitzvy bakers, bless them!

I was telling a group of New York women about our bar-mitzvah bakers when one of them said, "Hmmm, here we pay for our own bar mitzvahs!" She must have thought that I came from a community of *schnorrers*. She was wrong. You can't get bar-mitzvah bakers by begging or pleading, and certainly not by paying for them.

Happy is the mother who is blessed with a pride of bar-mitzvah bakers. Her status in the community is immediately established. She can go on for years, or at least until her next bar mitzvah, boasting of "the women who baked for me." As a matter of fact, if she has another bar mitzvah coming up, she had better keep boasting!

The mother has every reason to be proud, because money cannot buy the services of the women who bake for bar mitzvahs, although other things can.

Who are these warm, loving, generous souls who bring you the finest gifts of their kitchens? Some are your fellow Mah-jongg players. They bake for you because they are your friends, and because, for over a year now, you've been *nudyin* them, saying, "Who will bake for me? What will I do?"

In order to shut you up, they say, "So we'll bake already. What do you want from us!"

You tell them what you want from them, and how many.

Then there are those women who bake because next year will be by them! They are, in effect, taking out bar-mitzvah insurance. It's their policy. They pay the premiums now, next year they'll collect.

Many kindhearted souls bake because they've tasted your cakes. "I'll bake her a cake," they say, "so she'll know what a cake *is*!"

Then there are the women you hardly know. Maybe you know them well enough to say "*gut Shabbos*" or "*gut yom tov*" when you see them in the synagogue. They bake hundreds of cookies for you . . . in order you should invite them to the reception following the reception. The reception in the synagogue doesn't count. That's for everyone. At night you'll have the *real* reception, the one for your intimate friends—four hundred of them.

When I bake for bar mitzvahs, I have no ulterior motives. Sons I don't have, so I don't need insurance. I bake out of the warmth of my heart. After all, my strudel is so good, why shouldn't everybody have the pleasure of enjoying it? Of course, there are women who will say that I didn't start bar-mitzvah baking until after my grandson was born. Don't listen to them. There are belittlers in every community.

If, six years from now, there are women who remember my kindness by baking for my grandson's bar mitzvah, naturally, I won't deny them the pleasure. And those women who forget, I'll remember!

❤ 8 ❤

Mitzvah Bars

Did you ever hear of such a thing as Mitzvah Bars? To tell you the truth, I didn't either, but my friend Bessie, when she eats these delicious bars, always sighs with pleasure and says, "M-m-m, it's a *mitzvah* to give such cookies!" So I'm making up the name Mitzvah Bars. Who's going to stop me? Bessie also says, "Writers can get by with anything." She means me, because what other writer would Bessie know?

If you ever attend a bar mitzvah in Louisville, Kentucky, look around all the tables until you find the apricot bars made by Mrs. Yandell (Ann) Bush. But please, don't let on what you're doing! Walk around casual-like, stopping now and then to say, "Everything looks too beautiful to eat!" When you come to the apricot bars, have one. You'll want more, but don't take or you won't have room for the other wonderful treats, and if you'll hurt the feelings of the other bah-mitzvy bakers, I won't know who you are.

APRICOT BARS

⅔ c. dried apricots
½ c. butter
¼ c. sugar
1 c. sifted flour
⅓ c. sifted flour
½ tsp. baking powder
¼ tsp. salt
1 c. brown sugar, firmly packed
2 eggs, beaten
½ tsp. vanilla extract
½ c. chopped nuts

Rinse apricots. Place in a saucepan and cover with water. Bring to a boil. Boil 10 minutes. Drain apricots, cool, and chop or grind. Reserve.

Mix butter, sugar, and 1 cup flour until crumbly. Pat into bottom of greased 8-by-8 pan. Bake at 350° until lightly browned, about 20-25 minutes.

Sift together ⅓ cup flour, baking powder, and salt. Gradually beat brown sugar into eggs. Add the flour mixture and blend well. Stir in vanilla, nuts, and apricots. Spread over baked layer. Bake 25-30 minutes. Cool in pan. Cut into 1-by-2-inch bars. Serve plain or, if you're making for a bar mitzvah or a wedding and you want it should be real fancy, roll it in confectioners sugar so no one should know what it is.

It's been a long time since David Sagerman of Louisville, Kentucky, was a bachelor, but he calls these luscious, brownie-type cookies Bachelor Bars because they're so easy any bachelor can make them.

BACHELOR BARS

¼ lb. unsalted butter
1 c. graham cracker crumbs
6 oz. flake coconut
1⅓ c. condensed milk
1 c. nuts, finely chopped
6 oz. semi-sweet chocolate morsels

Melt butter in a 13-by-9-by-2 baking pan. Sprinkle graham cracker crumbs evenly over the bottom of the pan. Cover with coconut. Sprinkle with nuts, then chocolate morsels. Cover all with condensed milk.

Bake at 350° for 20 minutes. Cool. Cut into squares or bars.

Zara Finster of Hazard, Kentucky, says, "When my son William Howard was bar mitzvah, I baked five hundred of these apricot bars. Hazard never saw such a bar mitzvah!" Her recipe follows:

APRICOT BARS

¼ lb. butter
½ c. sugar
2 eggs, separated
1 tsp. lemon extract
1 c. flour
1 tsp. salt
½ tsp. baking soda
1½ c. apricot preserves
¼ c. sugar
½ c. chopped nuts
Confectioners sugar

Cream butter and ½ cup sugar. Blend in egg yolks and lemon extract. Sift together flour, salt, and soda. Add this to the creamed mixture, working in thoroughly. (This makes a sticky mess, but don't worry, it will be delicious.) Spread this evenly over the bottom of a lightly greased 8-by-12 pan. Cover with preserves.

Beat egg whites until fluffy. Continue beating while slowly adding ¼ cup sugar. Beat until stiff. Fold in nuts. Spread over preserves. Bake at 350° until light brown, about 40-45 minutes. Remove from oven. Dust with confectioners sugar. Cut into bars. (For the family make big, but if you want fancy, make small.)

Mrs. Max Keil makes her home in Wilmington, Delaware, where she has long been prominent in community and philanthropic activities. Rose Kluger Keil is the mother of nine children and the author of a novel, *A Woman Called Chaye*. Of her recipe for Cherry Coconut Bars, she writes, "We always double this recipe for organization affairs, and it never loses its flavor."

CHERRY COCONUT BARS

1 c. unsifted flour
½ c. soft butter
2 Tbs. confectioners sugar
¼ c. unsifted flour
2 eggs, beaten
½ c. granulated sugar
½ tsp. baking powder
¼ tsp. salt
1 tsp. vanilla extract
¾ c. chopped nuts
½ c. flaked coconut
½ c. maraschino cherries, well drained, or candied cherries

Mix 1 c. flour, butter, and confectioners sugar until well blended. Spread over the bottom of an 8-by-8 pan. Bake at 350° for 20 minutes.

Mix remaining ingredients. Spread carefully over the top of the baked mixture. Return to oven. Bake until done, about 25 minutes. Cool and cut into 1-by-2 bars or 2-by-2 squares.

A de-liteful and de-licious cooky recipe from Ann Bush.

CHOCOLATE DE-LITE BARS

½ c. butter
1 egg yolk
2 Tbs. water
1¼ c. flour
1 tsp. sugar
1 tsp. baking powder
6 oz. butterscotch morsels
6 oz. semi-sweet chocolate morsels
2 eggs
¾ c. sugar
6 Tbs. melted butter
2 tsp. vanilla extract
2 c. nuts, finely chopped

Beat butter, egg yolk and water until well blended. Stir in flour, 1 teaspoon sugar and the baking powder.

Press into a greased 13-by-9-by-2 pan. Bake at 350° for 10 minutes. Remove from oven. Immediately sprinkle with butterscotch and chocolate morsels. Return to oven for 1 minute. Remove from oven and smooth the melted morsels. Beat 2 eggs. Add sugar. Stir in melted butter and vanilla. Spread this over the chocolate-butterscotch layer. Sprinkle with nuts.

Bake at 350° 35-40 minutes. Cut into small squares.

Mrs. Ira (Sarah) Trivers was one of the co-editors of a cookbook published a few years ago by the Women's Auxiliary of the Chattanooga (Tennessee) Jewish Community Center. This recipe for delectable Coconut Bars is one of several that she shares with us.

COCONUT BARS

½ c. shortening
½ tsp. salt
½ c. brown sugar
1 c. sifted flour
1 c. brown sugar, firmly packed
1 tsp. vanilla extract
2 eggs, well beaten
2¼ Tbs. flour
½ tsp. baking powder
1½ c. shredded coconut
1 c. walnuts, coarsely chopped

Cream shortening with salt and ½ cup brown sugar. Blend in 1 cup sifted flour. Pat into a greased 8-by-12 pan. Bake at 325° until delicately brown, about 15 minutes.

Add 1 cup firmly packed brown sugar and vanilla to 2 well-beaten eggs. Blend well. Stir in remaining ingredients. Spread over baked layer and return to oven for 20 minutes. Cool and cut into small bars.

Mrs. Ronald (Lucille) Kaplan of Louisville, Kentucky, provides the recipe for these rich but easy-to-make date bars. Lucille finds it easy to collect recipes . . . and cakes, too. She's the chairman of the Altrusa Club's annual cake sale for the benefit of Kosair Crippled Children's Hospital.

DATE BARS

1 c. flour
1 c. sugar
1 tsp. baking powder
Pinch of salt
3 eggs
1 c. (8 oz. pkg.) dates, cut up
1 c. nuts, coarsely chopped
Confectioners sugar

Sift together flour, sugar, baking powder and salt. Stir in eggs. Fold in dates and nuts.

Bake at 350° in greased 9-by-13 pan until brown, 20-25 minutes. Cool. Cut into bars or squares. Roll in confectioners sugar.

Mrs. David (Judith) Halpern's Dream Bars won first place in the cooky division of the Louisville B'nai B'rith Women's Bake-off.

DREAM BARS

½ c. butter
1 c. flour
2 Tbs. brown sugar
2 eggs, well beaten
1½ c. brown sugar, loosely packed
¼ c. flour
½ tsp. baking powder
1 tsp. vanilla extract
1 c. chopped nuts, shredded coconut, or semi-sweet chocolate bits

Melt butter. Mix with 1 cup flour and 2 Tbs. brown sugar. Pat into the bottom of an ungreased 8-by-8 or 9-by-9 pan. Bake at 350° for 15 minutes.

Mix remaining ingredients. Spread over baked layer. Return to oven for 30 minutes. Cool. Cut into bars or squares.

Ann Bush is so fond of baking that she uses a commercial-size electric mixer to whip up tasty treats for her friends. Here's another of her recipes:

DREAM BARS

½ c. soft butter
½ c. brown sugar
1 c. sifted flour
2 eggs
1 c. brown sugar
1 tsp. vanilla extract
1 c. chopped dates
1 c. shredded coconut
1 c. chopped nuts
¼ tsp. salt

Mix the soft butter with ½ cup brown sugar and the flour. Press into a greased 8-by-8 pan. Bake at 350° for 15 minutes.

Beat together eggs and 1 cup brown sugar until light. Stir in remaining ingredients. Spread over baked layer. Return to oven for 20 minutes. Cut into bars or squares while still warm.

Mrs. George (Lee) Elkin of Los Angeles found this recipe in her mother's files. She writes, "For years I've used this recipe for happy occasions such as bar mitzvahs, *Oneg Shabbots,* or just for the pleasure of my guests. It is easy to make and provides a good 'pickup' sweet."

MOTHER'S DREAM BARS

½ c. shortening*
½ c. brown sugar
1 c. flour
2 eggs
1 c. brown sugar
1 c. chopped walnut
1 tsp. vanilla extract
1 c. shredded coconut
2 Tbs. flour
1 tsp. baking powder

Mix shortening, ½ cup brown sugar and 1 cup flour to a crumbly texture. Pat into a buttered 7-by-11 pan. Bake at 375° for 10 minutes. Set aside to cool while preparing the second part of the recipe.

Thoroughly blend eggs and 1 cup brown sugar. Add remaining ingredients. Spread over baked layer. Return to oven. Bake until done, about 20-25 minutes. Cool. Cut into bars or squares.

*Mrs. Elkin uses part butter and part shortening.

"I hope y'all like my Pecan Bars," says Gay Frehlich of Nixon City, Texas. "We grow so many nuts in Texas that it's practically my patriotic duty to circulate this recipe."

PECAN BARS

¾ c. butter
3 Tbs. granulated sugar
1½ c. sifted flour
3 eggs, separated
2¼ c. light brown sugar
1 c. pecans, coarsely broken
½ tsp. vanilla extract
Confectioners sugar

Cream butter. Slowly add 3 Tbs. sugar and sifted flour. Pat into a 7-by-11-by-1½ pan. Bake at 375° until golden brown, about 20-25 minutes.

While first layer is baking, beat egg yolks. Add brown sugar and continue beating until mixture is thick. Add nuts and vanilla. Fold in stiffly beaten egg whites. Spread evenly over first layer. Return to oven until topping sets, about 25-30 minutes. Dust with confectioners sugar. When cool, cut into bars or squares. Y'all'll like 'em. They are yummy! They're even yummier after they've aged a day or two.

"Whenever there's a *b'rith* or bar mitzvah in these parts, I'm called on to bake my Meringue Bars," says Mrs. Israel Lightfoot of Pitcher, Oklahoma. "They're also a good way to say howdy to a new neighbor."

MERINGUE BARS

½ c. shortening
1 c. granulated sugar
2 eggs, beaten
1½ c. flour
¾ tsp. salt
1 tsp. baking powder
½ tsp. vanilla extract
1 egg white
1 c. light brown sugar, sifted
1 c. chopped nuts
½ tsp. vanilla extract

Cream together shortening and granulated sugar. Stir in beaten eggs. Sift together flour, salt and baking powder. Blend dry ingredients into creamed mixture. Stir in ½ teaspoon vanilla. Spread in a shallow 10-by-15-by-¾ pan. Beat egg white until stiff. Gently fold in sifted brown sugar and chopped nuts. Stir in ½ teaspoon vanilla. Spread this thinly over first layer. (You will think it can't be done, but keep at it.) Bake at 325° about 25-30 minutes. Cool slightly. Cut into bars.

❤ 9 ❤

The Etiquette of Bar-Mitzvah Baking

I don't know when we started having bar-mitzvah bakers or why. All I know is that in my community, bar-mitzvah baking is already a tradition. We in the South are very conservative. We don't like to break with any tradition that is to our advantage, so I imagine that bar-mitzvah baking will be with us until we find something better. And what could be better?

Through the years, this custom has acquired its own special etiquette, which goes something like this:

Friday morning, the day before the bar mitzvah, the mother goes to the social hall of the synagogue. Her car is loaded with all the silver trays she could borrow, and with all the cookies she has kept in her friends' freezers for months. Inside the hall, the custodian has already set up long tables and covered them with white cloths.

Mama has just time enough to put on an apron and start opening boxes when the Mah-jongg girls walk in all at one time because, in this test of true friendship, each wants to show herself the truest. The girls bring silver trays, paper lace doilies, and goodies.

Now the girls start to work. All the boxes are opened and the cakes and cookies are arranged on trays. In every group there is at least one artist. She doesn't arrange the trays, she rearranges them. She waits until almost all the trays have been placed on the tables; then she walks around like the foreman in a cooky factory. She changes cookies about; she changes trays. Every ten minutes she brings the bar-mitzvah mother to see her handiwork.

"Now, don't you think it looks better this way?"

The mother agrees. What else can she do? After all, this is volunteer labor.

The girls who arranged the trays in the first place now come to the mother. "Who does she think she is, changing everything around? It looked better the first way."

The mother agrees. What else can she do? "Don't pay any attention," she says. "You know how she is . . . but she means well."

In every group there is also a rememberer. She comes to the mother with a superior smile. "I knew you'd forget it. I just knew you would."

The mother turns white. By now she is so confused she can't remember what she is supposed to have forgotten. "Oh, my," she sighs, "what did I forget? Tell me, what did I forget?"

"Don't get so shook up," the rememberer says, "it's not so *gefehrlich*. I knew you'd forget, so I brought it." From her purse she takes a shaker of powdered sugar.

The mother, who has two shakers of powdered sugar in the kitchen, says, "What would I do without you?"

Now the rememberer is like a regular sugarplum fairy. She dances around sprinkling powdered sugar on everything, including the pickled herring. Tomorrow, the bar-mitzvah bakers will have to make the rounds like miniature cyclones, blowing the sugar off the goodies until they can recognize their own offerings. From the powdered sugar fallout alone you can gain weight.

All this time, the parade of bar-mitzvah bakers has been going on. The mother needn't have bothered to bring an apron, she has no time to work. Her place is in the receiving line. It is here that the drama of the bah-mitzvy baker, bless her, unfolds according to ritual.

The bah-mitzvy baker makes her way to the mother. She may be carrying a cake so tall that she can't be seen from behind it. The mother is impressed, but to be merely impressed is not enough; she must be positively overcome by the magnitude of the gift.

"This is a cake?" she asks. "This is a jewel!" she answers. She calls the Mah-jongg girls to witness.

"Did you ever in your life see such a cake?" No, they never had . . . not since the last bar mitzvah.

This is the cue for the bah-mitzvy baker to speak her lines. She knows them well. She knows the part she has to play and she's going to make the most of it. "Oh, it's nothing," she says, "only a little twenty-five-egg Sunshine Cake."

But, like every actor, she is anxious to pad her part. She shakes her head tragically. "I don't know what happened," she says. "All the time I bake such wonderful cakes. Today, for spite, it didn't turn out well."

To this, the experienced bar-mitzvah mother will reply, "If this is bad, what can be good?"

This, of course, is the proper reply. But you know how some women are – they don't know what's proper. If you tell a woman like this that the cake didn't turn out right, she'll say, "Oh, that's too bad."

The nerve of her! The *chutzpah*! For this woman I'm not baking any more Sunshine Cakes, I don't care how many bar mitzvahs she has!

❤ 10 ❤

So You Should Know What a Cake Is!

This Apple Cake from the files of Mrs. H. L. Hollander is really something different . . . and special. You'll find it aromatic, moist, delicious!

APPLE CAKE

4 c. apples, freshly peeled and diced
1 c. sugar
¾ c. chopped pecans

Mix the above and let stand for one hour. Stir often so that mixture forms its own juice.

3 c. flour
½ tsp. grated nutmeg or cinnamon
½ tsp. salt
2 tsp. baking soda
¾ c. corn oil
2 eggs, well beaten
1 tsp. vanilla extract

Combine dry ingredients and fold into apple mixture. Add oil, well-beaten eggs and vanilla. Stir by hand. Do not use electric mixer.

Turn batter into a greased and lightly floured 9-inch tube pan. Bake at 350° for 60-70 minutes.

An excellent economy cake with a very fine texture. Mrs. H. L. Hollander baked it as a Sabbath cake.

CHIFFON CAKE FOR SHABBOS

2 eggs, separated
1½ c. sugar
2¼ c. sifted cake flour
3 tsp. baking powder
1 tsp. salt
⅓ c. oil
1 c. milk
1½ tsp. vanilla extract
10½ oz. jar pineapple topping

Beat egg whites until frothy. Gradually beat in ½ cup of the sugar. Continue beating until very stiff and glossy. Set aside.

Into a large mixing bowl, sift together the remaining sugar, the flour, baking powder and salt. Add oil, half of milk, and vanilla. Beat 1 minute on medium speed of electric mixer (or 150 vigorous strokes by hand). Scrape sides and bottom of bowl constantly.

Add remaining milk and egg yolks. Beat 1 more minute or 150 hand strokes, scraping bowl constantly. Fold in meringue.

Pour into 2 greased and lightly floured 8-inch layer pans or one 13-by-9-by-2⅝ cake pan.

Bake at 350° 30-35 minutes for layers, 40-45 minutes for large pan. Cool. Split layers. Spread with pineapple topping. Top cake with pineapple topping. Keep refrigerated.

"I looked for something a little different to send you," wrote Mrs. Eliezer (Sali) Berkovitz of Skokie, Illinois. She found it! This Chocolate Fruit Torte has an unusual flavor. Left plain, it is a good family cake, nice to serve when someone drops in for tea. Dressed up with a special topping, it's an impressive party cake that will serve about twenty.

CHOCOLATE FRUIT TORTE*

12 egg yolks
1½ c. sugar
1 lemon, juice and grated rind
½ lb. sweet or semi-sweet chocolate, melted
1 c. thick applesauce†
1 tsp. cinnamon
1 tsp. ground allspice
2 rounded Tbs. flour
10 egg whites, stiffly beaten

Beat 12 egg yolks until thick. Add sugar gradually, while continuing to beat. Add lemon juice and grated rind, continuing to beat until thick and golden. Stir in melted chocolate, applesauce and spices. Beat until well blended. Fold in flour. Fold in the 10 egg whites, which have been stiffly beaten. Pour into a 12-inch spring form.

Bake at 300° 1 hour and 15 minutes. Turn off heat. Allow cake to cool in oven with door closed. When cool, sprinkle with confectioners sugar or frost with the following frosting:

FROSTING

2 oz. butter
4 oz. sweet chocolate, melted
1 oz. brandy or strong coffee
½ tsp. vanilla extract
½ c. confectioners sugar

Beat well in small mixer bowl. Spread on cold cake.

*Mrs. Berkovitz says that the torte tastes its best when three days old.

I have to take her word for it, since it didn't last that long at our home.

The torte may sink slightly in the center, but don't be depressed about the depression. Use it to your advantage. Fill it with whipped cream or pistachio ice cream decorated with chocolate shavings, or top it with fruits. If your guests mention calories, tell them that there are only two tablespoons of flour in it, but forget to mention the amount of chocolate.

† It is best to use thick, homemade applesauce. When using the commercial kind, drain it. A 15 oz. jar of applesauce, well drained, will make approximately a cupful.

"This chocolate cake," says Edna Shaw of Chattanooga, Tennessee, "is as much a part of my life as any memories of my childhood. My mother insisted that she got the recipe from her mother, and I really believe that it belonged just to our family. Some of my cousins loved it so much that they had a piece of it for breakfast each morning This however, was not allowed to me because everyone knows that it isn't good for you to eat chocolate in the morning." You'll find this one of the most luscious chocolate cakes you've ever eaten!

CHOCOLATE LAYER CAKE

1 c. milk
4 oz. unsweetened chocolate
¾ c. sugar
5 eggs, separated
1 c. sugar
1 c. cake flour
1 tsp. baking powder
Preserves — cherry or apricot

Heat milk and chocolate together until chocolate is completely dissolved and mixture is thick. Stir ¾ cup sugar into this mixture.

Beat egg yolks with the remaining cup of sugar. To this add the chocolate mixture.

Sift together flour and baking powder three times. By hand, fold dry ingredients alternatively with stiffly beaten egg whites into the egg-chocolate mixture.

Pour into 2 greased and wax-paper-lined 8-inch layer pans. Bake at 350° for 25 minutes. Cool. Put layers together with preserves. Top with unsweetened whipped cream or your favorite icing. Here are three to choose from.

QUICK MOCHA ICING

1 c. confectioners sugar
4 tsp. cocoa
1 Tbs. butter
Strong, hot coffee

Combine sugar and cocoa. Add butter and enough very hot, strong coffee to make of spreading consistency.

ANN BUSH'S SOUR CREAM ICING

3 Tbs. butter
2 oz. unsweetened chocolate
2 c. confectioners sugar
1 tsp. vanilla extract
½ c. (approx.) sour cream

Over low heat, melt butter and chocolate. Blend in confectioners sugar and vanilla. Add as much sour cream as needed to make the frosting of spreading consistency. Beat well until creamy.

MY FRIEND BESSIE'S CREAM-CHEESE ICING

8 oz. cream cheese
2 c. sifted confectioners sugar
1 egg yolk
2 oz. unsweetened chocolate, melted
1 tsp. vanilla extract

Cream together cheese and sugar. Add egg yolk, melted chocolate, and vanilla. Beat until smooth.

Mary (Mrs. Stephen) Hornung of Louisville, Kentucky, is a creative cook whose creativity pays off. Her Cradle Cake, an original recipe, was a winner in the 1952 Pillsbury Bake-off. This Danish Gold Cake, however, is from a traditional recipe.

DANISH GOLD CAKE

2 Tbs. sweet butter
2 Tbs. fine bread crumbs
½ lb. sweet butter
1½ c. flour
5 eggs
1 ⅓ c. sugar
1¼ tsp. baking powder
¼ tsp. salt
1 tsp. almond extract

Prepare a 9-inch tube pan by greasing with 2 tablespoons of butter and dusting with bread crumbs. Cream together butter and flour. Add eggs, one at a time, beating after each addition. Slowly add sugar while continuing to beat. Stir in baking powder, salt and almond extract.

Pour into prepared pan. Bake at 325° until it tests done, about 40-50 minutes.

In 1958, Mrs. Louis B. (Celia) Marks was co-chairman of a cookbook committee for the Women's Auxiliary of the Chattanooga Jewish Community Center. The book they compiled, *Cook's Tour*, was a sellout. Since then, Celia has become food columnist for *The Chattanooga Times*. Her flavorful column enjoys a host of devoted readers. Here is one of her delicious recipes.

DATE CAKE

1 c. dates, cut fine
1 c. boiling water
½ c. butter
¾ c. sugar
1 tsp. vanilla extract
2 tsp. lemon juice
1 egg
1⅔ c. sifted flour
1 tsp. baking soda
¼ tsp. salt
½ c. coarsely chopped walnuts

Cover dates with boiling water. Set aside. Cream together butter and sugar until light and fluffy. Add vanilla, lemon juice and egg. Blend well.

Sift together flour, baking soda and salt. Add this to the creamed mixture alternately with dates. Beat well. Stir in nuts. Pour into a greased 8-by-12 Pyrex baking dish. Bake at 325° for about 45 minutes. Check for doneness after 40 minutes. When cake tests done, turn off heat and allow cake to remain in oven 5 minutes longer. Cake may be glazed while warm.

GLAZE

1 Tbs. melted butter
¾ c. (approx.) confectioners sugar
1 to 2 Tbs. orange juice
Few drops of lemon juice

Add sugar and fruit juice alternately to butter, using just enough sugar to reach a pouring consistency.

Betty Levine can testify that this hearty dessert is a favorite of growing boys. She used to mail two Fruit Tortes each week to her son's college fraternity for its Sunday-night treat. You'll not only marvel at the taste of this torte, you'll marvel at how she could have mailed it!

FAVORITE FRUIT TORTE

1 c. sugar
1 c. shortening
2 whole eggs
1 egg yolk
4 c. sifted flour
3 tsp. baking powder
½ c. orange juice
2 cans (1 lb. 4 oz.) pie filling cherry, apple, peach, etc.
1 egg white, slightly beaten
¼ c. sugar
½ c. chopped nuts

Cream together sugar and shortening. Add eggs and egg yolk, one at a time, beating after each addition.

Mix together flour and baking powder, and add to creamed mixture alternately with orange juice.

Roll or pat half of dough into an 11-by-15-by-½ cookie pan. Spread pie filling over dough. (If you like a fruitier torte, use 3 cans of filling. These fillings may be the same or different fruits, dividing the torte into thirds.) Cover with the remaining dough. No matter what method you use for adding the second layer, you'll end up with gaps in the dough. Don't worry, it will all come together like a family to a Bar Mitzvah. Brush with slightly beaten egg white. Sprinkle with sugar and nuts. Bake at 350° until lightly browned, 40-50 minutes.

Sarah Silverman of Roanoke, Virginia, sends the following recipe for a cake that is as light as its name:

FEATHER CAKE

½ c. butter
2 c. sugar
4 eggs
3 c. cake flour
4 tsp. baking powder
¼ tsp. salt
1 c. milk
1 tsp. vanilla extract

Cream butter. Add sugar gradually, continuing to cream. Add eggs, one at a time, beating after each addition.

Sift together flour, baking powder and salt. Add to creamed mixture alternately with milk. Add vanilla. Beat just enough to blend. Pour into two greased and lightly floured 9-inch layer pans. Bake at 375° 30-35 minutes. Frost with favorite frosting.

Easy to make and an excellent dessert is this cake from the files of Mrs. Dave (Elizabeth) Cohen of Central City, Kentucky.

FRUIT COCKTAIL CAKE*

2 c. flour
2 c. sugar
2 tsp. baking powder
1 tsp. baking soda
1 tsp. salt
2 eggs
No. 2½ can fruit cocktail, well-drained
1½ to 2 c. brown sugar
½ c. chopped nuts

Put everything except the brown sugar and nuts into a mixing bowl. Mix just until blended. Grease and lightly flour a 13-by-9-by-2⅝cake pan. Cover the bottom of the pan with a mixture of the brown sugar and nuts. Pour the batter over this. Bake at 350° for 45 minutes. May be served warm with whipped cream.

*Since this contains no shortening, it is good for a low-cholesterol diet. Without the whipped cream, it makes a delicious *pareve* cake, that is, a cake that can be served after either a meat or a dairy dinner.

Mrs. Maurice Blate of Canton, Ohio, is a housewife who really enjoys cooking and baking. You'll like the old-timey flavor of this Ginger Cake.

GINGER CAKE

¾ c. butter
1 c. sugar
2 eggs
½ tsp. ground ginger
½ tsp. ground cloves
¼ tsp. ground allspice
¼ tsp. cinnamon
1 c. molasses
3 c. sifted flour
1 c. buttermilk
1 tsp. baking soda

Cream butter. Gradually add sugar, continuing to cream. Add eggs, one at a time, beating thoroughly after each addition. Blend in spices and molasses. Add flour alternately with buttermilk in which baking soda has been dissolved. Pour into a greased 9-by-13-by-2⅝ pan that has been lined with wax paper. Bake at 350°, until cake tests done, 45-50 minutes.

Lucille Kaplan went through her grandmother's "receipt book" to find the Black Coffee Cake that follows. The book merely listed ingredients, but with a little experimenting, she came up with a cake somewhat similar to honey cake, but richer and moister.

GRANDMOTHER'S BLACK COFFEE CAKE

1 c. butter
2 c. sugar
4 eggs
4½ c. flour
2 tsp. baking soda
1 tsp. baking powder
2 tsp. cinnamon
1 tsp. grated nutmeg
1 c. strong black coffee, cold
1 c. molasses
1 lb. raisins
1 lb. currants
1 lb. chopped nuts

Cream butter. Gradually add sugar, continuing to cream. Add eggs, one at a time, beating each addition. Sift together flour, baking soda, baking powder, cinnamon and nutmeg. Stir coffee into molasses. Alternately add flour mixture and molasses mixture to creamed mixture. Fold in raisins, currants and nuts. Bake in well-greased and lightly floured 10-inch tube pans at 350° for 35-45 minutes.

Mrs. Harvey Curtis (Lucille) Webster of Louisville, Kentucky, found this recipe in her mother's files. The hickory nuts give this cake a most delicious and unusual flavor.

HICKORY NUT CAKE*

¼ lb. butter
1 c. sugar
3 egg yolks, well beaten
1 c. milk
1½ c. flour
1½ tsp. baking powder
1 c. hickory nuts, finely chopped
2 egg whites, stiffly beaten

Cream the butter. Gradually add sugar, continuing to cream. Add the egg yolks, which have been beaten until light. Add the milk. Mix together the flour and baking powder, and fold into the creamed mixture. Stir in the nuts. Fold in stiffly beaten egg whites. Bake in a greased and lightly floured 9-by-9 cake pan at 350° until it tests done, about 40-50 minutes. Frost with White Mountain Cream.

*The only thing difficult about baking this cake is finding and shelling the hickory nuts. You won't often find them at the supermarket. When you do see them, buy a pound. It will take that much for one cup of nutmeats. Save them for a rainy day when your children are tired of TV, stereo, and assorted games and hobbies. When they ask you "What can I do?" tell them they can shell hickory nuts. This should keep them busy for at least an hour. The hickory nuts give this cake its unusual flavor, but if you can't find them or have no children to shell them for you, try black walnuts. Let me know how it turns out.

WHITE MOUNTAIN CREAM

1 c. sugar
⅓ c. water
1 egg white, stiffly beaten
½ tsp. vanilla extract

Boil sugar and water without stirring until it spins a thread (242°). Pour the syrup slowly onto the stiffly beaten egg white, continuing to beat. Add the vanilla and continue beating until creamy. Spread with a knife that has been dipped into hot water. If the frosting hardens before you have it all spread, add a little hot water.

Sarah Settle, descendant of a pioneer Kentucky family, recalls traveling to Arizona at the age of four. "We rode in the caboose of a train one day and a stagecoach the next," says Sarah, "to reach our new home, a copper-mining town high in the mountains." Home again in Louisville, she delights her friends with reminiscences and such Southern treats as beaten biscuits and the following Kentucky Pecan Cake from a recipe handed down by a great-aunt:

KENTUCKY PECAN CAKE

½ lb. citron
1 lb. raisins
1 lb. currants
½ lb. almonds
½ lb. English walnuts
1 lb. pecans
¼ c. (approx.) flour
1 c. butter
1 c. sugar
1 tsp. cinnamon
1 tsp. ground allspice
1 tsp. ground cloves
1 tsp. freshly ground nutmeg
6 eggs
½ c. molasses
½ tsp. baking soda
1 tsp. baking powder
3½ c. sifted flour
½ c. finest Kentucky bourbon

Prepare two loaf pans (9¼-by-5¼-by-2¾) by greasing, lining with brown paper, and greasing the brown paper.

In a very large mixing bowl (a roaster may be used) combine fruit and nuts. (If possible, use unblanched almonds. Use walnut and pecan halves unless economy dictates that you buy broken nut meats, but if economy were dictating you wouldn't be baking this cake.) Dust the fruit and nuts with about ¼ cup of flour.

In a *very, very large* mixing bowl, cream the butter. Add the sugar gradually, continuing to cream. Add spices and continue creaming until mixture is light and fluffy. Add the eggs, one at a time, beating well after each addition.

Heat the molasses just to a boil, remove from flame, and stir in baking soda. (Be sure to use a large enough saucepan, as you'll end up with twice as much molasses as you reckoned with.) Stir molasses into the creamed mixture. Stir the baking powder into the sifted flour and add alternately with the bourbon whiskey to the creamed mixture.

Fold in fruits and nuts, making sure that all are covered with batter. Pack well into prepared loaf pans.

Place pans on the middle rack of preheated 250° oven. Place a pan of water on the rack below. Bake 2½ to 3 hours.

Place pans on a cooling rack. When cakes are cool, remove from pans. Remove brown paper. Let cakes stand out uncovered for a day or two. Wrap cakes in plastic wrap and place in plastic bags. This cake improves with age and will keep indefinitely.

Mrs. Samuel Reinglass of Canton, Ohio, shares a number of her favorite cake recipes with us.

MAPLE NUT CAKE

½ c. shortening
1 c. dark brown sugar
2 egg yolks
1½ c. flour
¼ tsp. salt
2 tsp. baking powder
½ c. milk
1 tsp. vanilla extract
1 c. chopped pecans
2 egg whites, stiffly beaten

Cream together shortening and sugar. Beat in egg yolks. Sift together flour, salt and baking powder. Add dry ingredients alternately with milk to creamed mixture. Stir in vanilla and nuts. Fold in stiffly beaten egg whites. Pour batter into a greased and lightly floured 9-inch tube pan. Bake at 350° for 30-35 minutes, or bake in two 8-inch layer pans for 25-30 minutes. Cool and ice.

ICING

2 Tbs. hot milk
½ Tbs. butter
1½ c. confectioners sugar
½ Tbs. maple flavoring

Blend all ingredients. Beat until smooth.

The recipe for the following old favorite comes from Mrs. Maurice Blate:

MERINGUE SPICE CAKE

¾ c. butter
1½ c. brown sugar
3 eggs, separated
2 c. sifted cake flour
1½ tsp. cinnamon
⅜ tsp. salt
¾ tsp. baking soda
1½ tsp. baking powder
¾ c. buttermilk
¾ c. brown sugar
¾ c. nuts, coarsely broken

Cream butter. Add 1½ cups brown sugar, continuing to cream. Add egg yolks. Blend thoroughly. Sift together sifted flour, cinnamon, salt, baking soda and baking powder. Add to creamed mixture alternately with buttermilk. Beat egg whites until stiff. Gradually add ¾ cup brown sugar; continue to beat. Pour batter into lightly greased and floured 12-by-8 cake pan. Spread meringue over the top. Sprinkle with nuts. Bake at 350° about 50 minutes. If the meringue is browning too quickly, place a sheet of heavy brown paper on the rack above the cake.

For a light, fine-textured cake that reaches its peak of flavor when a few days old, try this recipe, which comes from Dinah R. Rosenblatt of Buffalo, New York.

MOCK POUND CAKE

1 c. butter
2 c. sugar
1 tsp. vanilla extract
1 tsp. lemon extract
4 eggs
3 c. sifted cake flour
½ tsp. baking soda
½ tsp. baking powder
¾ tsp. salt
1 c. buttermilk

Cream together butter, sugar and flavorings until very light. Add eggs, one at a time, beating after each. In an electric mixer, continue to beat at medium speed for 2½ minutes. Sift together dry ingredients and add alternately with buttermilk to creamed mixture. Beat an additional 3 minutes at medium speed. Bake in 2 greased loaf pans, 8½-by-4½-by-2½, at 325° for 70-75 minutes.

Another delicious cake from Edna Shawl:

ORANGE CAKE

¾ c. butter
1 c. sugar
2 eggs, separated
1½ c. cake flour
2 tsp. baking powder
⅛ tsp. salt
½ c. orange juice

Cream together butter and sugar. Add egg yolks and continue to beat until thick and lemon-colored. Sift together dry ingredients and add alternately with orange juice to the creamed mixture. By hand, fold in stiffly beaten egg whites. Bake in two lightly greased and floured 8-inch layer tins at 350° for 20 minutes. Cool. Spread filling between layers and ice with orange icing.

FILLING

6 Tbs. sugar
2 Tbs. cornstarch
Pinch of salt
¼ c. water
¾ c. orange juice
1 egg yolk, slightly beaten
1 (8¼ oz.) can shredded pineapple, drained
2 Tbs. butter

Mix sugar, cornstarch and salt. Gradually add water, orange juice and egg yolk. Beat with a rotary egg beater. Cook in double boiler until smooth and thick. Fold in pineapple and butter. Cool.

ORANGE ICING

2 Tbs. butter
5 Tbs. orange juice
2 c. confectioners sugar
1 Tbs. rum

Melt butter; add orange juice and bring to a boil. Pour over sifted confectioners sugar until almost the right consistency for spreading. Add rum. Icing should be fairly thin, since the cake is very light and crumbles easily.

Mrs. Samuel Reinglass finds this Orange Delight Cake a favorite with guests.

ORANGE DELIGHT CAKE

¾ c. shortening
1½ c. sugar
3 egg yolks
2¼ c. flour
½ tsp. salt
3½ tsp. baking powder
¾ c. cold water
¼ c. orange juice, combined with 1 Tbs. grated orange rind
3 egg whites, stiffly beaten

Cream together shortening and sugar. Blend in egg yolks. Sift together flour, salt and baking powder. Add alternately with water, orange juice and rind to the creamed mixture. Fold in stiffly beaten egg whites.

In 9-inch layer pans which have been greased and lightly floured, bake at 350° until they test done, 30-35 minutes. Cool on rack. When cool, spread the following filling between layers:

FILLING

2 Tbs. butter
¾ c. cornstarch
1 c. sugar
½ tsp. salt
1 c. orange juice and pulp
2 Tbs. grated orange rind
1½ Tbs. lemon juice

Melt butter in top of double boiler. Blend in cornstarch. Add sugar, salt, orange juice, pulp and rind. Blend well.

Cook until thick. Remove from fire. Add lemon juice. Beat well. Cool. Spread between cake layers. Frost with the following:

ORANGE FROSTING

¾ c. sugar
¼ c. water
2 egg whites, stiffly beaten
½ Tbs. orange juice

Cook sugar and water, without stirring, until it spins a thread (242°). Slowly pour this syrup over stiffly beaten egg whites while continuing to beat. Stir in orange juice. Continue beating until smooth and creamy.

Mrs. Louis R. Myers of Canton, Ohio, sends a recipe that her sister, Pauline Cook of Baltimore, Maryland, inherited from her husband's family. "It is an elegant cake for very special occasions," she says, "and is famed throughout many Southern states."

PAULINE COOK'S CAKE

1 c. butter
1 c. granulated sugar
1 c. dark brown sugar
4 eggs, separated
4 c. flour
3 heaping tsp. baking powder
1 tsp. ground allspice
1 tsp. ground cloves
1 tsp. cinnamon
1 tsp. grated nutmeg
1 c. light cream
½ c. dark molasses
¼ lb. citron or orange peel
½ c. grated bitter chocolate
1 c. chopped nuts
2 c. raisins

Cream together butter with sugars. Add egg yolks. Sift together dry ingredients and add alternately light cream to the creamed mixture. Stir in molasses. Fold in citron, chocolate, nuts and raisins. Fold in stiffly beaten egg whites. Bake in 3 greased and lightly floured 9-inch layer pans at 375° 25-30 minutes. Cool on racks. Remove from pans. Put layers together with the following filling:

FILLING

3 c. brown sugar
1 c. light cream
1 Tbs. butter
½ tsp. vanilla extract

Combine ingredients, except vanilla, in a saucepan. Bring to a boil. Boil until a little dropped in cold water forms a soft ball (236°). Remove from flame. Add vanilla. Beat just until creamy. If it becomes too thick, it may be thinned out with a little cream. Spread quickly between layers.

Minnie (Mrs. Raymond) Gertz of Cranston, Rhode Island, married her high-school sweetheart. They now have five children, ranging in age from seven to fourteen. "It is difficult to find something all seven of us like," says Minnie, "but this Pineapple Fluff Cake is a favorite with all. It's as light as a chiffon cake; besides, it fits into my covered cake dish for carrying to my sister's home."

PINEAPPLE FLUFF CAKE

6 egg whites
¼ tsp. salt
1½ c. sugar
6 egg yolks
1 Tbs. lemon juice
½ c. unsweetened pineapple juice
1½ c. cake flour
1 tsp. baking powder

Beat egg whites with salt to form moist, glossy peaks. Gradually beat in ¾ c. sugar. Beat egg yolks with rest of sugar until they are very thick and sugar has dissolved. Add fruit juices. Sift together flour and baking powder. Add to egg yolk mixture. Fold in egg whites. Bake in 10-inch ungreased tube pan at 350° for about 50 minutes. Invert to cool.

Sarah Trivers suggests that we take particular notice of the unusual baking method for this delicious Pound Cake.

MY BEST POUND CAKE

1 lb. butter
2⅔ c. sugar (reserve 6 Tbs.)
8 eggs, separated
3½ c. sifted flour
8 Tbs. light cream
1 tsp. vanilla extract
1 tsp. lemon extract
6 Tbs. (reserved) sugar

Cream together butter and sugar (less 6 Tbs.). Add egg yolks, 2 at a time, beating well after each addition. Add flour, light cream, vanilla and lemon extracts. Beat egg whites until foamy. Gradually add 6 Tbs. of sugar, continuing to beat until stiff. Fold egg whites into first mixture. Pour into a lightly greased and floured 10-inch tube pan. Set cake into a cold oven. Set thermostat at 350°. Turn on heat. Bake for 15 minutes. Reduce heat to 300°. Bake until cake tests done, a total of about 1 hour and 10 minutes. Let stand in pan 10 minutes before turning out.

From a farm near Michigan City, Indiana, comes this recipe for Pound Cake, the favorite of the Leon Kohns and their three sons. Mrs. Kohn, "Frenchy," says that her real name, Frances, has been lost for years. "My dad wanted to nickname me 'Fagel' (little bird) when I was a baby," says Mrs. Kohn, "but Mother wanted Frenchy. She won." The Kohns raise chickens "so the eggs for this cake cost us more this way, but we like it." They like it best in summer when, once a week, the Kohn clan gathers. Mr. Kohn is one of a family of five brothers and sisters, all living in the same area. The family gatherings number "twenty-nine or so." When it's Frenchy's turn to have the family, the Pound Cake is called for. A former big-city girl, Frenchy vows she'll never leave the farm.

POUND CAKE

1 c. butter
1½ c. sugar
1 tsp. vanilla extract
3 eggs, beaten
3 c. sifted flour
1½ tsp. baking powder
½ tsp. salt
¼ rounded tsp. mace
½ c. milk

Cream butter. Add sugar, continuing to cream until well blended. Add vanilla. Add eggs and beat well. Sift together flour, baking powder, salt and mace. Add alternately with milk to the creamed mixture, beating well after each addition. Pour into a greased 10-inch tube pan. Bake at 350° about 40-50 minutes. The cake should be brown, and will split on the top when done. Cool in the pan. This cake is at its flavor peak about three days after baking.

This old Southern recipe comes from Mrs. Louis R. (Minna) Myers of Canton, Ohio, who terms it a "fine courtesy cake," excellent to take to shut-ins or to say hello to a new neighbor. "It is truly a 'y'all' cake," says Mrs. Myers, "since our family comes from below the Mason-Dixon line. My home was originally Maryland. I have always been proud to consider myself from the Southern States, where cooking is an art, and baking a pleasure."

PRUNE CAKE

¾ c. butter
1½ c. sugar
4 eggs
2½ c. sifted flour
2 Tbs. cocoa
1 tsp. cinnamon
1 tsp. grated nutmeg
½ tsp. salt
½ tsp. baking powder
1 scant tsp. baking soda
1 c. prunes, cooked, pitted and cut up
1 c. chopped nuts
½ c. unsweetened prune juice (more, if batter is too stiff)

Cream together butter and sugar. Add eggs, one at a time, beating after each. Sift together all dry ingredients into the creamed mixture. Fold in until all is moist. Fold in prunes and nuts. Stir in prune juice. Bake in two greased, lightly floured 9-inch layer cake pans at 350° for 30-35 minutes. Cool and ice.

ICING

1 lb. confectioners sugar
¼ lb. butter
Grated peel and juice of 1 orange

Cream together butter and sugar. Add orange peel and juice. Beat until creamy.

An excellent cook, Mrs. Allan (Mariam) Mayer of Louisville, Kentucky, likes to share her favorite recipes with friends. The following is one of them:

PRUNELLA CAKE

½ c. butter
1 c. sugar
2 eggs
⅔ c. stewed prunes, pitted, drained and chopped
1⅔ c. sifted flour
½ tsp. baking powder
½ tsp. baking soda
½ tsp. salt
½ tsp. cinnamon
½ tsp. nutmeg
½ tsp. ground allspice
⅔ c. sour milk
Damson plum jam*

Cream together butter and sugar. Add eggs, beating well after each. Fold in prunes. Sift flour, measure and resift with baking powder, soda, salt and spices. Add to creamed mixture alternately with sour milk. Beat until smooth. Pour into two well-greased 8-inch layer-cake pans. Bake at 375° until it tests done, about 25 minutes. When cake is cool, remove from pans and spread jam between layers. Cover top and sides with Uncooked Frosting.

UNCOOKED FROSTING

2 Tbs. butter | **⅛ tsp. salt**
2 c. sifted confectioners sugar | **2 Tbs. prune juice**
½ tsp. cinnamon | **1 tsp. lemon juice**

Cream butter until soft. Gradually add confectioners sugar. Blend until creamy, then add cinnamon, salt, prune and lemon juices.

* The plum jam is my own idea, but if you think it's painting the lily, you're entitled to your own opinion.

Different, delicious, and not-at-all pumpkinish-tasting is Pumpkin Cake from Mrs. Herbert (Naomi) Charlip. A young Syracuse housewife and mother of four, Naomi decided that the best place to use a home-economics degree was in her own home. Here is her recipe:

PUMPKIN CAKE

3 c. flour
2 tsp. baking soda
2 tsp. cinnamon
2 tsp. baking powder
1 tsp. salt
2 c. sugar
1 c. oil
No. 303 can pumpkin-pie filling
4 eggs
1 tsp. vanilla extract
½ c. nuts, chopped
½ c. raisins

Into a large mixing bowl, sift together all dry ingredients. Make a depression in the center. Into this depression put oil, pumpkin, eggs and vanilla. Stir until smooth. Fold in nuts and raisins.

Bake at 350° in ungreased loaf pans for 1 hour, or in 9-inch tube pan about 1½ hours. Dust with confectioners sugar or ice with the following:

CARAMEL ICING

9 Tbs. light-brown sugar
9 Tbs. evaporated milk
3 Tbs. butter
1 tsp. vanilla extract
2 or 2½ c. confectioners sugar

Bring sugar, milk and butter to a boil. Remove from flame. Add vanilla and enough confectioners sugar to make of spreading consistency. Beat until smooth.

Bella Smith of Milwaukie, Oregon, finds the following cake, adapted from an old Yankee recipe, excellent for a kosher kitchen. It makes a fine *pareve* (suitable with meat or dairy dinner) dessert. "I like to make this cake when I'm baking bread," says Bella, "because it is quick, easy, and economical."

RAISIN CAKE

1 c. hot water
1 c. raisins
1 c. sugar
⅓ c. oil
2 c. flour
1 tsp. cinnamon
Pinch of ground cloves
½ tsp. nutmeg
1 tsp. baking soda
½ tsp. salt
¾ c. chopped nuts

In a large saucepan, boil together for 5 minutes hot water, raisins, sugar and oil. Remove from flame. Sift together into the saucepan, flour, spices, soda and salt. Blend well. Fold in chopped nuts. Pour into a greased and lightly floured 9-by-9 cake pan. Bake at 350° until it tests done, about 25-30 minutes.

As a busy interior designer and the "mother of three children and a dog," Marian (Mrs. Sanford) Sachs requires that her excursions into the kitchen be rewarding—and they are. Her guests never leave a crumb of this unusual torte.

ROYALE CHOCOLATE TORTE

CINNAMON MERINGUE SHELL

2 egg whites
¼ tsp. salt
½ tsp. vinegar
½ c. sugar
¼ tsp. cinnamon

Beat egg whites, salt and vinegar until they form soft peaks. Blend together sugar and cinnamon and gradually add to egg whites while continuing to beat. Beat until very stiff. Place a piece of heavy brown paper on a cookie sheet. Draw an 8-inch circle on the paper. Spread meringue on the circle, hollowing out center and building up sides.

Bake at 275° for 1 hour. Turn off heat and allow to dry in oven for 2 hours. Peel from paper and fill:

FILLING

6 oz. semi-sweet chocolate pieces
2 egg yolks, beaten
¼ c. water
1 c. heavy cream
¼ c. sugar
¼ tsp. cinnamon
Whipped cream and pecan halves for garnish

Melt chocolate pieces over hot (not boiling) water. Cool slightly. Spread 4 tablespoons melted chocolate over the bottom of the cooled meringue shell. Add egg yolks and water to the remaining chocolate. Blend and chill until thick. Combine cream, sugar and cinnamon. Whip until stiff. Spread half the whipped-cream mixture over the chocolate in the shell. Fold the rest into the remaining chocolate and spread over the top. Chill several hours or overnight. Garnish with whipped cream and pecan halves. Serves 8-10.

If you want people should talk . . . so bake this cake! They won't stop raving about its color and taste. The recipe comes from Mrs. Carl (Irene) Starr of Louisville, Kentucky.

RED VELVET CAKE

½ c. shortening
½ c. sugar
2 Tbs. cocoa
1 tsp. vanilla extract
2 eggs
2 oz. red food coloring
2½ c. cake flour
1 tsp. salt
1 c. buttermilk
1 tsp. baking soda
1 Tbs. vinegar

Cream together shortening, sugar, cocoa and vanilla. Add eggs, one at a time, beating after each addition. Add 2 ounces red food coloring. Beat well. Sift together flour and salt. Stir baking soda and vinegar into buttermilk. The buttermilk will bubble up, so be sure to have it in a large enough container. Add flour and buttermilk alternately to creamed mixture, beginning and ending with flour. Bake in two 8-inch layer pans which have been greased and lightly floured. Bake at 350° until it tests done, about 30 minutes.

When cakes have cooled, split the layers. Put the four layers together with the following icing between:

ICING

5 Tbs. flour
1 c. milk
1 c. butter
1 c. sugar
1 tsp. vanilla extract

Cook together flour and milk, stirring constantly until thick and smooth. Set aside to cool thoroughly.

Cream together butter, sugar and vanilla. Slowly add to the cooled milk mixture. Beat until smooth and fluffy.

"The girls in Texas wouldn't be caught dead without a pecan pound cake in the home," says Mrs. Milton C. Davis, now of Louisville, Kentucky. The wife of an Air Force lieutenant colonel, she has lived in many sections of the country and has made a hobby of collecting regional recipes. Mrs. Davis finds the Texas Pecan Pound Cake a very versatile cake. It can be served plain or with strawberries or ice cream or both. It may even be toasted and served with marmalade for morning coffees.

TEXAS PECAN POUND CAKE

1 c. butter
½ tsp. salt
2 c. sugar
4 eggs
3 c. sifted flour
1 c. fresh buttermilk
¼ tsp. baking soda
1 tsp. vanilla extract
1 tsp. lemon extract
1 c. chopped pecans

Cream together butter, salt and sugar. Add eggs, one at a time, beating well after each addition.

Add flour (saving out a small amount with which to dust the pecans) alternately with buttermilk. Stir soda into the last ⅓ cup of buttermilk and add to batter. Add extracts. Fold in the flour-dusted pecans.

Bake in a greased 9-inch tube pan at 300° until it tests done, about 60 minutes. Cool for 10 minutes. Remove from pan.

"Every time my Aunt Dora came to see me," says Minnie Gertz, "she brought a Tomato Soup Cake. Our family liked it so much, I asked her for the recipe."

AUNT DORA'S TOMATO SOUP CAKE

1 c. sugar
2 oz. shortening or butter
½ tsp. salt
1 egg
1 can (10¾ oz.) tomato soup
1 tsp. baking soda
½ c. raisins
½ c. chopped English walnuts
1½ c. flour
1 tsp. cinnamon

Blend sugar and shortening. Add salt and egg.

Open can of tomato soup, mix baking soda in it. Add to the first mixture. Fold in raisins and nuts.

Sift together flour and cinnamon. Fold into first mixture. Bake in 9-inch tube pan at 350° for 50-60 minutes. Cool. Sprinkle with confectioners sugar.

Lucille Kaplan gives us another of her grandmother's "receipts."

WHIPPED CREAM CAKE

1 c. whipping cream
2 eggs
1 c. sugar
1 tsp. vanilla extract
1½ c. sifted cake flour
¼ tsp. salt
2 tsp. baking powder

Whip cream until it holds its shape.

Beat eggs until thick and lemon-colored. Add to whipped cream. Whip until light and foamy. Add sugar and beat again. Add vanilla.

Sift together sifted flour, salt and baking powder three times. Fold into egg mixture.

Bake in greased and lightly floured 8-inch layer pans at 350° until cake tests done, 25-30 minutes. Cool. Frost with whipped cream.

From the files of Mrs. H. L. Hollander:

WHITE CAKE

⅔ c. butter
1 c. sugar
1½ c. flour
¾ c. milk
1 tsp. vanilla extract
5 egg whites, stiffly beaten
½ c. flour
1 tsp. baking powder

Cream butter slowly. Gradually add sugar. Continue creaming until light and fluffy.

Add 1½ cups flour alternately with milk to the creamed mixture. Add vanilla. Beat very well.

Carefully fold in stiffly beaten egg whites.

Sift ½ cup flour with baking powder. Add this to the first mixture. Stir well, *but do not beat.*

Bake in two greased and lightly floured 8-inch layer pans at 325° until cake tests done, about 35 minutes. Let cake stand 5 minutes before removing from pan. Frost with Seven-Minute Frosting.

SEVEN-MINUTE FROSTING

2 egg whites
1½ c. sugar
5 Tbs. water
1½ tsp. light corn syrup
1 tsp. vanilla extract

Combine egg whites, sugar, water and corn syrup in the top of a double boiler. Beat with a rotary egg beater until thoroughly blended.

Place over rapidly boiling water. Beating constantly, cook for seven minutes or until frosting will stand in peaks.

Remove from boiling water, add vanilla, and beat until thick enough to spread.

Shredded coconut or chopped nuts may be added to the frosting.

11

There's Nothing Like a Bar Mitzvah

My friend Bessie says that there's nothing like a bar mitzvah, not even a wedding! She only says this because I have no sons, and because it gives her another opportunity to tell me what a wonderful bar-mitzvah speech her Joe made.

"Bessie," I say to her, "don't recite the speech again. I was there, remember?"

"How can I remember?" says Bessie. "It was all like in a dream."

"If it was all like in a dream, Bessie," I say, "so how come you still remember who baked for you, and, more important, who didn't?"

Bessie makes like she doesn't hear. "Do you remember how he made the blessing over the challah?" says she. "It's years already, and people are still talking. The Hebrew words fell from his lips like pearls."

"What greater occasion is there than a Sabbath dinner?" asks June Konigsberg, who sends us her own recipe for Shabbos Challah. June, who lives in Sierra Madre, California, says, "My husband and I developed this recipe over a period of several months . . . starting from a standard recipe. The smell of the baking bread is half the fun . . . Chanel No. 5 could be ashamed!" June starts making the bread about two o'clock on a Friday afternoon, so that it comes out of the oven about six p.m., with the warm fragrance there to greet her husband when he comes home to Sabbath dinner.

CHALLAH
(*Sabbath Twist Loaf*)

¼ tsp. sugar
¼ c. lukewarm water
1 pkg. dry yeast
5 c. flour
2½ tsp. salt
2⅓ Tbs. sugar
1 Tbs. oil
1 egg plus 1 egg yolk, beaten
1½ c. warm water (approx.)
1 egg white
1 Tbs. water
Pinch of sugar

Dissolve ¼ tsp. sugar in ¼ cup warm water. Sprinkle dry yeast into water. Let stand about 10 minutes.

In a large bowl, mix together flour, salt and sugar. Make a well. To the well add oil, the egg and egg yolk (which have been beaten) and dissolved yeast and approximately 1½ cups warm water. (Add part of the water, adding the remainder if necessary to moisten all the flour.) Knead until smooth and elastic. Form dough into a ball. Place on floured board. Cover and let rest for 25-30 minutes. Knead again. Place in a greased bowl. Cover and let rise until doubled in bulk, about an hour. Punch down.

Divide dough into 3 equal parts (a kitchen scale comes in handy here) for braiding. Braid loaf. Place on a greased baking sheet. Cover. Let rise until doubled in bulk, about an hour. Brush with egg white, which has been slightly beaten with 1 tablespoon water and a pinch of sugar.

Bake at 350° for 1 hour. Breathe in the aroma. Taste. Enjoy!

If you listen to Bessie, you think, really, that there was no bar mitzvah like Joe's. But if you ask me, they're all nice. At some bar mitzvahs there are more people, at some less. A few people one way or the other doesn't mean anything, but if more than a few people stay away, it's practically a social disgrace for the family.

When this happens, I blame the mother. After all, it's up to her to invite people. I don't mean she should send everyone engraved invitations, but I do say that for weeks she should be on the telephone calling people. For weeks, every time she goes to the supermarket, to a Sisterhood meeting or to Hadassah or Mizrachi, she should say to everyone she meets, "Don't forget our bar mitzvah, I specially want *you* to be there." If she will do this she is sure to have a nice crowd, because everyone knows that it's a *mitzvah* to attend a bar mitzvah, especially if you're invited.

So who comes to a bar mitzvah? All the relatives, naturally, down to the third and fourth cousins, even the ones you're not talking to. All the out-of-town relatives who can afford the fare, and some who can't, will come. They will say to themselves, "How many opportunities do we have to see all the relatives together? Isn't it better to go for a *simcha,* a joyous occasion, than, God forbid, something else?"

Who else will be there? Your friends, of course. Some will come from a great distance, so that you can say when you see them, "Now this is a friend!"

Then there are those people who go to synagogue on Saturday morning anyway. What can you do? You can't tell them to stay away. Why should you? Your son is so bright, why shouldn't everyone have the pleasure of hearing him?

I don't know how it is in your community, but in ours, unfortunately, we have still another type of bar-mitzvah guest. I call them the Pioneers. They follow the bar-mitzvah trail from synagogue to synagogue! They are members of another congregation, but they come anyway. Can you blame them? When the bar mitzvah is called up to read the day's portion of the Torah, the Pioneer will nudge his neighbor. "So who's the boy?" he will ask.

At the appointed time, the bar-mitzvah recites a carefully memorized speech. In the days of the *shtetl*, the Eastern European Jewish community, this was an elaborate oration, a *drosheh*, a discussion of some Talmudic problem, an interpretation of the law. Nowadays, it is usually a simple speech in which the bar mitzvah expresses his gratitude to his parents, his grandparents, his rabbi and teachers, and all those who have so lovingly brought him to this first plateau of manhood.

The boy's mother and all his female relatives shed a few tears. They are as proud as if the boy had written the speech himself. Perhaps he did, but most likely the rabbi wrote it for him. You see, the rabbi knows this kid and he's not about to trust him with expressions of gratitude. Perhaps he feels that the lad has not had enough experience.

The ceremony ends with the rabbi giving the boy his blessing. Before this, he has given him a little sermon telling him of his responsibilities to his parents, to his community, to his nation, and to his faith. In effect, he has said, "Today you are a man and must assume the greater responsibilities of manhood."

The youth's first act of manhood is to ask his father for a larger allowance with which to meet these increased responsibilities.

Now that the religious rites are over, the Pioneers wake up. It is time for the reception in the social hall. The rabbi has asked that the congregation remain seated until the bar mitzvah and his family have left the sanctuary. But the Pioneers are seated strategically near the doors, so does it hurt if they go out first? If you wait until later, there is such a mob that you can't get near the strudel. Besides, if you're slow, you may be forced to go through the receiving line, and without a glass of *schnapps* and a piece of *kichel*, who has the strength to go through such a long line? After you've had a bite to eat and wrapped a few goodies in a paper napkin to "take home for the children," then will be time enough to give the bar-mitzvah family a *mazel tov*.

The Pioneers wait only until the bar mitzvah has recited the blessing over the Sabbath loaf; then they make a dash for the sweet table for a piece of strudel. Do you think they can get it? No. Standing around the table is the guard of honor, the bar-mitzvah bakers.

You reach for a piece of strudel, but before you can touch it, Mrs. Cohen is making with her head "no."

"You're reaching for the strudel?" says Mrs. Cohen. "Don't take. Mrs. X baked. Feh! It's all covered with icing you shouldn't know how bad it is."

"So what's good?" you ask.

"You want to know what's good? You want to know what's really good?"

Naturally, you want to know.

"Go round the table," says Mrs. Cohen, "You'll find my chocolate-covered *eier kichel*. They're out of this world!"

* * *

These *Kichlech* are the real old-time favorites. The recipe comes from Mrs. Isadore (Rose) Goldstein of Louisville, Kentucky. Rose learned her Southern hospitality up north . . . she's a transplanted Canadian who loves to give big parties for which she does all the cooking and baking. Dissatisfied with the conventional kitchen work space, Rose designed a large square worktable with utility drawers around the sides. Three women can work at this table with ease. It proved a boon when her Canadian relatives, all excellent cooks, came to help her prepare for her son's bar mitzvah. Rose and her husband relax on their farm which they have named Ga-Naden (Paradise).

EIER KICHLECH

3 eggs **½ c. oil**
Pinch of salt **⅞ c. (approx.) sifted flour***
1 Tbs. sugar **Sugar for sprinkling**

Beat eggs in electric mixer at No. 8 speed until very thick and lemon-colored. Add salt and sugar while continuing to beat. Gradually add oil while continuing to beat.

Continue beating while sifting and measuring flour. Add flour, several tablespoons at a time, beating after each addition until smooth. Batter should be spongy but not rubbery, and should be thick enough not to spread when dropped from spoon. Remove bowl from mixer. With long, slow strokes of a fork, beat air into batter for at least 5 minutes – the longer, the better.

Drop batter from a teaspoon on to a lightly greased cooky sheet, one inch apart. Batter should be thick enough so that it must be pushed from the spoon with the finger. Sprinkle liberally with granulated sugar. Bake at 325° until golden brown, about 25-30 minutes. If you are successful, these will come out feather-light, with a deep cavity in the back.

* The amount of flour needed may vary with different brands.

This recipe for traditional Eier Kichel comes from Mrs. K. Cohen of Roanoke, Virginia.

EIER KICHEL

2 eggs **2 tsp. lemon juice**
1 Tbs. sugar **1 tsp. vanilla extract**
½ tsp. salt **1½ c. flour (approx.)**

Beat eggs well. Add sugar, salt, lemon juice, vanilla, and enough flour to form an easy-to-handle dough.

Knead lightly. On lightly floured pastry board, roll out to ⅛-inch thickness. Cut into diamond shapes about 3 inches long. Fry in deep, hot oil (350°) until lightly brown. These brown very quickly and should be turned shortly after dropping into oil. Drain on brown paper. Sprinkle with confectioners sugar.

"I always have Kichel on hand," says Trudy Emmes of Missoula, Montana, author of the following recipe. "It goes so well with a glass of wine for the Sabbath *kiddush*."

KICHEL

3 c. unsifted flour
1 heaping Tbs. shortening, melted
7 eggs, slightly beaten
Pinch of salt
Granulated sugar

Put flour into a large mixing bowl. Make a depression in the center into which put eggs, shortening and salt. Knead well. This will make a sticky dough, but more flour will be absorbed in the rolling.

Pinch off a portion of dough, form into a ball and roll out very thin on a well-floured pastry board. Sprinkle generously with sugar. Roll sugar in with a rolling pin. Quickly cut into diamond shapes. Do not allow the sugar to stand on the dough for long. Place on a baking sheet. Bake at 375° until toast-brown around the edges, about 10 minutes.

❤ 12 ❤

An Engagement is a Happy Occasion No Matter What

"An engagement is a happy occasion no matter what," said my friend Bessie when I told her I was writing a bake book for happy occasions.

"You ought to have it in your book," Bessie went on; when Bessie starts talking she always goes on. "You ought to have it in your book because an engagement should be celebrated no matter what."

"What do you mean, no matter what?" I asked.

"What do I mean no matter what?" said Bessie. "I mean no matter what. If I meant something else I would say something else and a certain party would spread it all over town that I don't like David, that his family isn't good enough, and that I think they're both too young."

"*Mazel tov*, Bessie," I said. "*Mazel tov!* The best of luck to them. So why didn't you tell me? I'm your best friend and you don't say a word. You probably called everyone already."

"Thank you for your good wishes," said Bessie, "and don't get touchy with me because you know how I like when people get touchy with me. It happened only last night. It's not yet official, and if I felt like calling anybody I would have called you first. I was going to tell you, but the minute you stepped in the door you started talking about your book, and when you start talking . . ."

That's the way Bessie is. Every fault she has she puts off on me. I've got enough faults of my own without taking on hers. This time I let it drop. I'm not the kind of person who likes to start arguments—at least not on a happy occasion like this.

"Children, that's what they are," Bessie was saying, "Just children. What do they know about life? And they want to get married yet!"

"So what will you do?"

"What can I do?" said Bessie. "I'll make an open house to celebrate the happy occasion."

My friend Bessie is never right about anything, but about this she was right. An engagement should be celebrated if only for one of two reasons—either because you feel like celebrating, or because you want people to think you feel like celebrating. And as long as you're giving a party, it should be a nice one. After all, you don't want the *machetenista*, your daughter's new mother-in-law, to think that you don't even know how to give a party. This is your time to show her. It's a lot of trouble, but it's worth it.

The *machetenista* should call to offer her assistance, and then leave town. From now on, nothing she does will be right. Even leaving town is wrong, but if she's going to be wrong, it's better to be wrong at a distance.

"She left town already," said my friend Bessie, a week after she had informed me of the engagement.

"Who left town?"

"You know who," said Bessie. "Her Majesty Queen Victoria. Queen Elizabeth she's not! I'm killing myself making this party and she goes away for a rest."

"Maybe she needs it."

"Who says she doesn't? From playing Mah-jongg every day you can get tired too."

"She didn't offer to help?"

"Sure she offered," said Bessie. "Sweet as sugar she offered. You'd think I didn't know how to give a party without her."

There's one thing I'll say for my friend Bessie, she knows how to give a party. Her cakes are beautiful to look at. I knew that if I came around often enough and listened to her complaints long enough, she'd give me her prize recipes. I got a lot of recipes from her, it's true, but don't think I didn't work for them. I listened to all her complaints. She was still complaining the day of the party when I came over with all my silver trays, platters, and bonbon dishes.

"She called yesterday," Bessie said, "and don't say 'Who?' because you know already who. She's back from her rest cure. She could have stayed another day. She didn't have to come back just to ask me if I needed her silver. Like I don't have silver! I thanked her very kindly and told her that I have enough silver for two parties. Then she said, 'I would like to do *something*. Couldn't I send a floral centerpiece for the table?'"

"That was nice," I said. "She really does want to help."

"Look how dumb you are," said Bessie. "She was trying to tell me, in a nice way, of course, that there should be a centerpiece for the table. As if I didn't know."

All of which may lead you to believe that a *machetenista* can never win, but you're wrong. Bessie's party was a great success. The *machetenista* herself told Bessie so. She also praised Bessie's cooking to the skies, and said how lucky her son was to get into such a fine family. It turned out, too, that she didn't play Mahj every day, only twice a week. She invited Bessie to join her Mah-jongg club. Now they are the best of friends, which is why I say that Bessie was right when she said that engagements should be celebrated, no matter what.

ENGAGEMENT-TYPE COOKIES

Mrs. Lewis Conn is co-publisher, with her husband, of a weekly newspaper. When she isn't "putting the paper to bed, you may find her promoting dramatic activities at the Louisville Jewish Community Center. She has never lost interest in the theater since the time when, as Irene Fox, she enjoyed a long run in the Broadway hit "Pins and Needles." Irene still finds time to bake such treats as these Almond Horns.

ALMOND HORNS

½ lb. butter
5 Tbs. sugar
2 c. flour
1 c. blanched almonds, chopped

Cream together butter and sugar. Work in flour, a little at a time, until thoroughly blended. Stir in almonds. Dust hands with flour. Pinch off small pieces of the dough. Roll the dough between the palms of your hands to form a rope about 1½ inches long, thicker at the center (about little-finger width) than at the ends. Place on a cookie sheet. Pull ends toward center to form a crescent. Bake at 375° until light beige in color, about 10 minutes. Remove from oven. Roll in confectioners sugar. Makes about 100.

"I may not leave footprints on the sands of time," says Mrs. R. B. (Liz) Browning of Pippa Passes, Kentucky, "but my Thumb Prints, both Cherry and Chocolate, can be seen at every b'rith or bar mitzvah in these parts. They're a favorite at hootenannys, too!"

CHERRY THUMB PRINTS

¼ c. shortening
¼ c. butter
¼ c. light brown sugar
½ tsp. vanilla extract
1 egg yolk
½ tsp. salt
1 c. sifted flour
1 egg white, slightly beaten
1 c. finely chopped nuts
Maraschino cherries*

Cream together shortening, butter and sugar. Blend in

vanilla, egg yolk and salt. Gradually work in flour until thoroughly blended. Using a level teaspoon as a measure, roll dough into balls. Dip balls in slightly beaten egg white, then roll in finely chopped nuts. Place on baking tin, an inch apart. Bake at 375° for 5 minutes. Remove from oven. Quickly and gently press thumb into center of each cookie. Return to oven for 8 minutes. Cool. Fill each center with half a maraschino cherry.

* Tinted confectioners sugar icing may be used in place of cherries.

More of Liz Browning's Thumb Prints! If you're careful to get the balls of dough all the same size, they'll look like bakery-made! But where will you find a bakery that can make them taste so good?

CHOCOLATE THUMB PRINTS

½ c. butter
½ c. light brown sugar
1 tsp. vanilla extract
1½ c. sifted flour
½ tsp. salt
2 Tbs. milk
¼ c. semi-sweet chocolate bits, chopped
Confectioners sugar

Cream together butter and sugar. Blend in vanilla. Sift together flour and salt and work into creamed mixture. Stir in milk and chocolate bits.

Form into 1-inch balls. Place an inch apart on baking tin. With your thumb, make a depression in the center of each ball. Bake at 375° 10-12 minutes. Remove to platter. Dust with confectioners sugar, and fill thumb prints with the following:

FILLING

¾ c. semi-sweet chocolate bits
1 Tbs. shortening
2 Tbs. light corn syrup
1 Tbs. water
1 tsp. vanilla extract

Melt chocolate bits and shortening over hot water. Remove from heat. Stir in corn syrup, water and vanilla. Cool for 5 minutes. Fill thumb prints.

Irene Conn's Cinnamon Nut Crisps are a favorite at parties, but if you're feeling antisocial, so save them for your own afternoon coffee breaks. After all, where is it written that every time you bake a batch of cookies you have to give a party?

CINNAMON NUT CRISPS

½ lb. butter
1 c. sugar
1 egg separated
2 scant c. flour
4 tsp. cinnamon
1 c. pecans, finely chopped

Cream together butter and sugar. Beat in egg yolk. Work in flour and cinnamon until thoroughly blended.

Press dough onto a 13½-by-9½-by-½ cookie sheet. Brush with unbeaten egg white. Sprinkle with chopped nuts.

Bake at 350° until slightly brown around the edges, about 25 minutes. Cut into diamond shapes while still hot.

"The women here in Galena, Kansas, take such pride in their baking," says Mrs. Doffman Cannon, "that I was beginning to get an inferiority complex. I had our cook teach me how to make Delcas. Now there's no need for me to learn anything else, my Delcas are in such demand!"

DELCAS

½ lb. butter
3 c. flour
1 tsp. salt
1 cake yeast
1 pt. commercial sour cream
2 egg yolks
½ c. sugar mixed with
1 tsp. cinnamon
1 c. chopped nuts

Blend butter, flour, salt and yeast with a pastry blender or fork. Blend in sour cream and egg yolks. Cover. Refrigerate overnight. Divide dough in 6 parts. Work with one part at a time, keeping remainder refrigerated. On a lightly floured pastry board, roll dough to a thin 8- or 9-inch circle. Dust with cinnamon-sugar mix. Sprinkle with nuts.

Cut into 8 wedges. Starting at the broad base, roll up each wedge. Place point down on a cookie sheet. Pull ends toward center to form a crescent.

Bake at 425° until golden brown, about 8-10 minutes. Dust with confectioners sugar when cold.

"From me you are expecting a French recipe, non," writes Mrs. Jacques (Cheri) Goldberg of Paris, Kentucky. "These croissants you will find *delicieux, mais oui*!"

FRENCH PASTRY CRESCENTS

½ lb. butter
½ lb. creamed cottage cheese
2 c. flour
Apricot preserves
Confectioners sugar

Blend butter, cottage cheese and flour. Knead dough with hands until thoroughly blended. Form into a ball. Wrap in wax paper and refrigerate over night.

When ready to bake, cut ball into 8 equal wedges. Work with one portion at a time, keeping remainder refrigerated. Form wedge into a ball and on lightly floured wax paper (adding flour when necessary to keep dough from sticking), roll out into an 8-inch circle. Spread with apricot preserves. Cut into 8 pie-shaped wedges.

Starting at the broad base, roll up each wedge. Place, point side down, on baking tin. Pull sides down to form crescents. Bake at 425° for 5 minutes. Reduce heat to 350° and bake until golden brown, 10-12 minutes. Remove to platter. Dust with confectioners sugar.

At bar-mitzvah and wedding receptions, you'll want to brighten your cooky trays with Ann Bush's Fruit Slices. They may be too pretty to eat, but eat them anyway. From the bourbon alone you'll be happy!

FRUIT SLICES

4 eggs
½ c. sugar
¾ c. sifted flour
½ tsp. salt
1 tsp. baking powder
1 lb. pitted dates (whole)
¾ lb. brazil nuts (whole)
¾ lb. English walnut halves
16 oz. jar maraschino cherries, drained
¼ c. flour
¼ c. cherry juice, mixed with
⅓ c. Kentucky bourbon

Beat eggs. Gradually add sugar. Blend in flour, which has been mixed with salt and baking powder. Set aside. Put dates, nuts and maraschino cherries into a large mixing bowl. Coat with ¼ cup flour. Add the batter and mix (by hand) until all the fruits and nuts have been coated with batter. Grease two loaf pans (approximate size 10-by-3½-by-2½) and line bottom and sides with wax paper. Fill the pans about half full. Bake at 250° for 2 hours.

Remove cakes from pans and place on cake racks. Peel off wax paper immediately. Cool about 10 minutes. Spoon mixture of cherry juice and bourbon over cakes. Allow cakes to cool completely. Slice them. Pack slices with wax paper between layers. Freeze until ready to use.

"These Twists are a special favorite of my children," says Mrs. Meyer (Minnie) Siskin of Chattanooga, Tennessee.

GERMAN SOUR CREAM TWISTS

3½ c. sifted flour
1 tsp. salt
1 c. shortening (part butter or all margarine)
1 cake yeast
¼ c. lukewarm water
¾ c. sour cream
1 egg plus 2 egg yolks
1 tsp. vanilla extract
1 c. sugar (for rolling)

Into a large mixing bowl, sift together flour and salt. Cut in shortening. Dissolve yeast in lukewarm water and stir into flour mixture. Stir in sour cream and well-beaten egg and egg yolks. Stir in vanilla. Knead well until thoroughly blended. Cover with a damp cloth and refrigerate for 2 hours. On a sugared pastry board, roll out half of the dough to an 8-by-16 rectangle. Fold the upper part of dough to the center. Fold the lower section to overlap the upper section. Sprinkle with sugar. Roll out again to the same size. Repeat the process twice. Cut into strips 1-by-4 inches. Hold strip at both ends and twist in opposite directions, stretching slightly. Place strips, in the shape of a horseshoe on ungreased cooky sheet. Bake at 350° until golden brown, about 15 minutes. Remove from tin immediately. Yield, about 5 dozen.

Mary Hornung makes these Hungarian cookies in the old-time way by mixing them directly on her pastry board, but if you find this method too difficult, just use a mixing bowl.

HARD-BOILED EGG COOKIES

2¼ c. flour
½ lb. sweet butter
½ c. sugar
4 hard-boiled egg yolks
3 raw egg yolks
½ lemon, juice and grated rind
2 egg whites, lightly beaten
1 c. sugar, mixed with
1 c. walnuts, coarsely chopped

Place flour on the center of a pastry board. Gradually work in butter by rubbing between the fingertips. When the butter and flour are well blended, make a well.

Into the well pour the sugar. With the tines of a fork press the hard-boiled egg yolks into the sugar. In the same manner, add the lemon juice and rind and the raw egg yolks. Cut the butter-flour mixture into the well mixture with a knife. Finally, gently knead with hands.

Roll out to about ¼-inch thickness on a lightly floured board. Cut with small cooky cutter. Brush tops with lightly beaten egg white. Dip brushed side of cooky into mixture of chopped walnuts and sugar.

Bake on ungreased cooky sheet at 375° until lightly golden on bottom, about 12 minutes.

Mrs. Clarence (Suzanne) Claugus, homemaker, mother, and chemist, is as adept in the kitchen as she is in the laboratory. What's more, the results taste better. Suzanne, a native Hungarian, has not forgotten how to make fine Hungarian pastries such as the following:

HUNGARIAN BUTTER WREATHS

½ lb. butter
2½ c. flour
¾ c. sugar
2 egg yolks (reserve whites)
⅓ c. sour cream
1 Tbs. rum
Grated rind of ½ lemon
1 c. blanched almonds
10 lumps of sugar
Raspberry jelly

Work butter into flour. Add sugar, egg yolks, sour cream, rum and lemon rind. Divide dough in half. Form into two balls, cover, and let stand in cool place for 2 hours or overnight.

Cut blanched almonds into fine slivers. (Commercially slivered almonds must be further slivered.) Break the sugar lumps coarsely and mix with almonds in a shallow dish. In another shallow dish, whip reserved egg whites with a fork.

On a lightly floured pastry board (if you're a slow worker, roll out on lightly floured wax paper) roll out about ⅛ inch thick. Cut out cookies with a 1½-inch cutter. Using a thimble, cut hole in the center of half of the cookies. Brush "holed" cookies with beaten egg white and turn into almond-sugar mixture so that the top is well covered with nuts. Place nut-covered cooky on top of plain cooky. Place on buttered cooky sheet and bake at 375° until golden brown, about 15-20 minutes. Remove from oven. Place a small amount of raspberry jelly in each hole.

From one of the great cooks of Chattanooga, Tennessee, Mrs. Clarence (Edna) Shaw, comes this recipe for Kipfel. Says Edna, "As you know, Kipfel are typically Viennese, but when I ate them in Vienna, they were not as good as those my mother made, and neither are mine. Since the dough must be kept cold while being rolled, Mother never made them in the summertime. She would use only a large marble board for rolling. How she got the pastry as thin and flaky as it was and still thick enough to encase the filling completely, I'll never know. But, undaunted, I keep trying, and things are getting better. Don't think that Kipfel are really as difficult to prepare as I seem to be implying. One gets the knack very quickly and the result is, by all means, worth the effort."

KIPFEL

2 egg yolks (reserve whites)
1 c. commercial sour cream
2½ c. flour, sifted
½ c. sugar
½ lb. butter
Softened butter (for rolling pastry)

Mix together egg yolks and sour cream. Set aside.

Mix together sifted flour and sugar. Cut in butter with a pastry blender until granulated. Add egg-and-sour-cream mixture. Blend until smooth. Cover and chill overnight. (Dough may be kept chilled for a week.)

When ready to bake, cut off ¼ of the dough, keeping remainder refrigerated until ready to use. Roll very thin on a floured pastry board. Roll lightly or dough will stick. (If you're heavy-handed, perhaps you'd better roll out dough on a piece of floured wax paper.) Spread with softened butter. Fold over into thirds and roll out again as thin as before. Repeat this process two more times, spreading with softened butter each time. Roll out as thin as possible without tearing.

Cut into 3-inch squares. Spread with 1 rounded teaspoon of filling and roll up tightly, as for a jelly roll. Pinch ends to seal. Seal edge with slightly beaten egg white. Place, sealed side down, on ungreased baking sheet, and form into crescents.

Bake at 400° for 5 minutes. Reduce temperature to 350° and continue baking until pale golden in color, 15-20 minutes. Remove from baking sheet. Sprinkle with confectioners sugar while still hot. More confectioners sugar may be sifted on before serving.

FILLING

4 c. finely ground nuts, (½ walnuts, ½ pecans)	**4 Tbs. brown sugar**
½ tsp. grated lemon rind	**6 Tbs. granulated sugar**
½ tsp. grated orange rind	**12-15 vanilla wafers, crumbled**
5 Tbs. lemon juice	**6 Tbs. jelly**
5 Tbs. orange juice	**5 Tbs. cream**
	1 tsp. almond extract

Combine all ingredients. Filling should be moderately firm. More crumbled cookies (vanilla wafers or similar type) and ground nuts may be added if filling seems runny.

These not-too-sweet sweets that you'll want to eat by the dozen are a favorite of Elsie (Mrs. Edward) Sagerman of Millburn, New Jersey.

RUGGELACH
(*Yeast Horns*)

1 pkg. dry yeast	**3 egg yolks**
¼ c. lukewarm water	**½ lb. salt butter, melted**
3 c. flour	**1 can (6 oz.) evaporated milk**

FILLING

1 c. sugar mixed with	**1 c. chopped nuts**
2 tsp. cinnamon	**1 c. raisins**

Dissolve yeast in lukewarm water. Measure flour into a mixing bowl. Make a well in the center of the flour. Into the well, add the dissolved yeast, egg yolks, melted butter and evaporated milk. Blend into a dough. Divide dough into 2 parts. Wrap each part in wax paper and refrigerate overnight. When ready to bake, divide each half of dough into 3 equal parts. Roll each part into an 8- or 9-inch circle on a pastry board which has been sprinkled with ⅙ of the cinnamon sugar mix. Cut the circle into 8 pie-shaped wedges. Sprinkle with nuts and raisins. Starting at the broad base, roll up each wedge. Place, point down, on a lightly greased cookie sheet, and curve into a crescent shape. Bake at 300° until it feels firm to the touch, about 25-30 minutes.

"*Ah meichel im beichel,*" is what Mrs. Louis E. (Edith) Perlman says of her Southern Pecan Tartlets. Freely translated, this means "yummy in the tummy," and that's exactly what they are. Edith has been called the most magnificent bar-mitzvah baker of Temple B'rith Kodesh in Rochester, New York. She's also an excellent Yiddish comedienne. There's always plenty of *Gemütlichkeit* when Edith and her husband are around.

SOUTHERN PECAN TARTLETS

CREAM CHEESE DOUGH

¼ lb. salt butter
¼ lb. cream cheese
1 c. flour

Blend butter and cream cheese together. Work in flour until thoroughly blended. Refrigerate dough for several hours (may be kept in refrigerator for a long as 4 or 5 days). Remove dough from refrigerator ½ hour before using. Divide dough into 3 parts. Roll out each part on a lightly floured pastry board. Roll out rather thin, as for a pie crust. With a 2-inch cookie cutter, cut out into circles. Place circles in the cups of tiny muffin tins. Fill with the following:

FILLING

¼ lb. butter
1 c. sugar
2 eggs, separated
2 tsp. vanilla extract
1 c. chopped pecans
1 c. raisins

Cream butter and sugar thoroughly. Add egg yolks one at a time, beating after each addition. Stir in vanilla, pecans and raisins. Fold in egg whites which have been beaten until stiff, but not dry. Fill the shells ¾ full. Bake at 325° until filling is set, about 25-30 minutes. Remove tarts while still warm by cutting around the muffin tins very carefully with a small knife.

VARIATION: STRUDEL

You may use all or any part of this dough for strudel. Roll out very thin on lightly floured wax paper. Spread with jam, nuts, coconut, cinnamon-sugar mix, or any desired filling. Roll up tightly, as for a jelly roll. Place on a baking tin and bake at 350° for 35-40 minutes. While still warm, slice diagonally at 1-inch intervals.

Mrs. Leslie S. Cohen's Sugar Cookies were prize winners at the Louisville B'nai B'rith Women's Bake-Off in 1964.

SUGAR COOKIES

½ c. butter
½ c. sugar
1 egg
1 tsp. vanilla extract
1¾ c. flour
1 tsp. baking powder

Have butter at room temperature. Cream butter. Gradually add sugar while continuing to cream. Blend in egg and vanilla. Sift together flour and baking powder. Add to creamed mixture. This should make a dough that is easy to handle. Put through a cookie press to desired shapes. Decorate with maraschino cherries or nuts, if desired. Bake at 375° for 10-15 minutes.

The recipe for these Tiny Schnecken and Tartlets comes from petite Elise (Mrs. Walter) Lapp of Louisville, Kentucky.

TINY SCHNECKEN AND TARTLETS

1 cake yeast
¼ c. lukewarm water
1 c. evaporated milk, scalded and cooled
½ lb. butter, melted and cooled
3 egg yolks, beaten
3 c. flour, mixed with
3 Tbs. sugar
1½ c. sugar mixed with
1 Tbs. cinnamon
Melted butter
1 c. (approx.) finely chopped nuts
Preserves (for tartlets)

In a large mixing bowl, dissolve yeast in water. Add cooled milk and butter. Add beaten egg yolks. Add flour, which has been mixed with 3 Tbs. sugar. Stir only until all the flour is moistened. Cover. Refrigerate overnight.

FOR SCHNECKEN:

Remove ¼ of dough from refrigerator. It will be sticky. Roll out on wax paper which has been liberally sprinkled with cinnamon-sugar mix. Coat rolling pin with cinnamon sugar mix from time to time. Turn dough 3 or 4 times, so that both sides of dough will get sugar-coated. Roll to ⅛-inch thickness.

Brush with melted butter. Sprinkle with finely chopped nuts. Roll up tightly, as for jelly roll, making about 4 rolls (about ½ of sheet). Continue rolling process with the remaining half of sheet. Cut rolls into ½-inch slices. Place slices, cut side down, on greased cookie sheet. Flatten out gently with finger tips. Bake at 325° until delicately brown, 15-18 minutes.

FOR TARTLETS:

Roll out dough on cinnamon-sugar mix, as for Schnecken. Cut out rounds with a 2-inch scalloped-edge cookie cutter. Place in greased cups of tiny muffin tins. Fill with ½ teaspoon strawberry, raspberry, or apricot preserves. Bake at 325° until delicately brown, about 18-20 minutes. Allow to cool completely before removing from tins. Remove by carefully running a silver knife around the edge of the tart, and lifting from tin.

A creative individual, Betty Levine has named her goodies Twist Craze—1964. How about some Watusi cookies, Betty?

TWIST CRAZE—1964

3½ c. flour
½ lb. butter
Pinch of salt
1 cake yeast
3 eggs, well beaten
1 tsp. vanilla extract
½ c. (scant) lukewarm milk
½ c. sugar mixed with
1 tsp. cinnamon
½ c. finely chopped nuts

In a large mixing bowl, crumble together flour, butter, salt, and yeast. Add the beaten eggs, vanilla, and enough of the lukewarm milk to make a fairly firm dough. (If you've added a little too much milk and the dough is sticky, wrap it in wax paper and refrigerate for about 2 hours.)

Roll out to ¼-inch thickness on a pastry board sprinkled with cinnamon-sugar mix and nuts. Fold one side to the center. Overlap with the other side. Roll out again. Repeat this procedure twice. Cut into 1-by-3-inch strips. Twist strips once or twice. Place on ungreased cookie sheet. Bake at 350° until golden brown, about 15 minutes. Remove from tin immediately. Yield, about 5 dozen.

"These cookies," says Edna Shaw, "were the one claim to fame of *die kleine* Meyer, a gentle, shy little woman who stood no more than four and a half feet and who was a part of the Kaffee Klatch ladies who gathered at our home once every two weeks. Mother admitted that she got the recipe from her, but that was almost fifty years ago, and I always gave Mother direct credit for them."

VIENNESE WAFERS

1 c. butter
⅔ c. sugar
2½ c. sifted flour
⅛ tsp. salt
½ tsp. almond extract
¾ c. (3¼ oz. pkg.) blanched almonds, ground
¼ tsp. vanilla extract
Whole almonds or maraschino cherries, for decorating

Cream butter with an electric mixer. Add sugar slowly, continuing to cream well.

Add remaining ingredients, except whole almonds and cherries. Form into balls slightly smaller than a quarter. Place on greased cooky sheet. Press down with a fork, dipping it in flour frequently to prevent sticking. Decorate with an almond or half a cherry.

Bake at 350° until slightly brown, about 12-15 minutes. Remove from tin. Allow to cool for a few minutes. Dust with confectioners sugar. Makes about 5 dozen.

❤ 13 ❤

Grandchildren Are Always a Happy Occasion

"You're a writer," my friend Bessie said to me one day. Whenever she's displeased with me, Bessie tells me what I am. She thinks this explains me even if it doesn't excuse me. "You're a writer," she said, "and I am just an ordinary person. You won't find me in Who's Who or even in What's What."

"You couldn't be just an ordinary person," I said, "because if you were an ordinary person and a friend came to your home, you would offer her a cup of coffee at least, before you started criticizing her."

"Who's criticizing? Am I a critic that I should criticize? An ordinary person isn't supposed to criticize a writer. But even an ordinary person has ideas, and if you ask me, a writer should have better ideas than an ordinary person."

"And what is wrong with my ideas?"

"Who says there's anything wrong with them? They're just a little lopsided, that's all."

"What do you mean, lopsided?"

"What do I mean, lopsided? I mean lopsided, too much on one side, not enough on the other. I don't know how it is with writers and other important people," said Bessie, "but the average ordinary person is sometimes happy and sometimes sad."

"So what's that got to do with my writing?"

"You're writing a book about happy occasions, yes? If someone should read your book they would think that the only happy occasions are bar mitzvahs and weddings, and in between times we sit and cry. If you ask me, there are more happy occasions."

"So I'm asking you."

"Grandchildren are a happy occasion," said Bessie. "When they come safe into this world, we're happy. When they learn to walk or they learn to talk, what a pleasure it is! When you have their pictures to show to your friends, can you have a better pleasure? Let me tell you, when I bake cookies for my grandchildren and the little ones say to me, 'Grammommy, you're a good cooker!'—this is for me a very happy occasion."

My friend Bessie is very often wrong, but when she's right, she's right, and I have to agree with her. Grandchildren are always a happy occasion.

Grandchildren-type Cookies

Mrs. Maurice (Sylvia) Hyman of Nashville, Tennessee keeps busy teaching ceramics and creating blue-ribbon-winning ceramic sculpture, so she looks for short cuts when it comes to baking. These Brownies are short on work (use only one saucepan, so there's not much washing up to do) but long on taste. Her teen-age son and daughter think the Brownies deserve a blue ribbon, too.

BROWNIES

½ lb. butter
4 oz. unsweetened chocolate
4 eggs
2 c. sugar
1 c. flour
2 tsp. vanilla extract
1 c. chopped nuts

In a large saucepan, melt together butter and chocolate. Remove from flame. Add eggs, sugar, flour and vanilla. Stir until well blended.

Pour into a greased 9-by-13 cake pan. Sprinkle with chopped nuts. Bake at 350° for 25-30 minutes. Cut into squares.

"I bake these cookies for my grandchildren," says Hortense Goode of Van Buren, Arkansas. "With so many good things in them, how can they be bad (the grandchildren, not the cookies)?"

CHOCOLATE PEANUT CLUSTERS

½ c. shortening
½ c. butter
1 c. peanut butter (crunchy)
1 c. granulated sugar
1 c. dark brown sugar
2 eggs
2 c. sifted flour
1 tsp. baking soda
1 pkg. (6 oz.) chocolate morsels
½ lb. salted peanuts

Cream together shortening, butter and peanut butter. Gradually add sugars, continuing to beat until well blended. Add eggs, one at a time, beating after each addition.

Sift together flour and soda and add to creamed mixture. Fold in chocolate morsels and peanuts.

Drop from teaspoon on baking sheet. Flatten with a fork. Bake at 325° about 13-15 minutes. Makes about 6 dozen.

Mrs. Ben (Sara) Leventhal of Nyack, New York, finds her Cooky Rings a great favorite with her grandchildren.

COOKY RINGS

2 hard-boiled egg yolks
2 raw egg yolks
¾ c. sugar
¼ lb. butter, creamed
1 c. flour
1 egg white, slightly beaten
10-15 lumps of sugar, crushed

In a medium-size mixing bowl, crush the hard-boiled egg yolks with the tines of a fork. Add raw egg yolks. Stir in sugar. Alternately add well-creamed butter and flour, blending well after each addition. Cover bowl and refrigerate for 2 hours. Pinch off pieces of dough. Roll between the palms of the hands to form a rope about the size of your little finger and about four inches long. Form into a ring. Brush top of ring with slightly beaten egg white and dip in crushed lump sugar. Place on cooky sheet about one inch apart. Bake at 350° until lightly brown around the edges, about 10 minutes. Remove from cooky sheet immediately.

Here's a real grandchild-pleaser from the files of Mrs. Michael Zane.

DOUGHNUTS

¼ c. butter or shortening
1 c. sugar
2 eggs
1 tsp. vanilla extract
4 c. flour
4 tsp. baking powder
1 tsp. salt
1 tsp. ground nutmeg
½ tsp. cinnamon
1 c. milk

Cream together shortening and sugar. Add eggs, one at a time, beating after each addition. Add vanilla.

Sift together flour, baking powder, salt, nutmeg and cinnamon. Add to creamed mixture alternately with milk. Cover bowl and refrigerate for about 1 hour.

Turn dough out on floured board. Knead lightly. Roll out to ¼-inch thickness. Cut with a floured doughnut cutter. Lift doughnuts with a wide spatula and slide quickly into deep hot fat (375°). Turn doughnuts as they rise to the surface and show brown around the sides. Lift from fat with a long fork (do not prick doughnuts) slipped through hole. Drain for a second over kettle. Place on absorbent paper. When well drained, dust with confectioners sugar.

The recipe for these fast-disappearing sugar cookies comes from Mrs. Manning (Mildred) Bernstein, who is one of the two best Jewish cooks in Charleston, South Carolina. In 1950, when the Charleston Jewish Community celebrated its bicentennial, Mrs. Bernstein was chairman of the Banquet Arrangements Committee. She has at various times presided over the Sisterhood of historic Beth Elohim* Congregation, the National Council of Jewish Women, and the B'nai B'rith Women of Charleston, and served on the board of the National Jewish Hospital in Denver, Colorado.

SUGAR COOKIES

1 lb. butter
1 lb. 4X sugar
4 eggs
1 tsp. vanilla extract
1 tsp. lemon extract
8 c. self-rising flour
Melted butter
Coarse granulated sugar

Cream together butter and sugar. Add eggs one at a time, beating after each addition. Add vanilla and lemon extracts. Work in flour with your hands until all is thoroughly blended. Refrigerate overnight. When ready to bake, take out a small amount of dough at a time, leaving remainder refrigerated. Roll out thin on a lightly floured pastry board. Cut with a 2-inch cookie cutter. Place on ungreased cookie sheet. Brush lightly with melted butter and sprinkle with coarse granulated sugar. Bake at 375° until brown around the edges, about 6-8 minutes. This recipe yields more than 12 dozen cookies. Even if you don't have children or grandchildren to steal from your cookie jar, these crisp lemony cookies will disappear in no time at all!

* Temple Beth Elohim was established in 1750. The original synagogue, destroyed by fire in 1838, was described by Lafayette as "spacious and elegant." A prized possession of Temple Beth Elohim is a letter from George Washington to the congregation.

❤ 14 ❤

A is a Happy Occasion

"What I don't understand," my friend Bessie said to me one day, "is how come you think you know all about happy occasions?"

"Did I say I know all about them?"

"You didn't come right out and say it, but when you write a book about happy occasions, that means you think you know more about them than anyone else. I'm not a writer, I'm just an ordinary person, and I tell you that you don't know."

"Bessie," I said, "when you give me this ordinary-person routine, I know already that everything is wrong. So don't play games with me. I haven't got all day."

"You see?" said Bessie. "That's your problem. You don't take time to listen and to learn. You're always busy, busy, busy. You don't have time to listen to your friends."

"What's the matter with you, Bessie?" I said. "Didn't I listen to you? Didn't I put into my book grandchildren like you said?"

"So now, by accident, I learn that I'm in the book," said Bessie. "You couldn't give me the satisfaction to tell me? All right, I forgive you. You've got things on your mind And as long as I'm in the book once, so maybe you'll put me in twice."

"You didn't tell me yet what's wrong with the book."

"It's not so terrible," said Bessie. "I see you already have the most important things. Of course, they're all big occasions like you make a party for. Sometimes people can be happy with little things. Sometimes, even, a friend gives good advice, it's a happy occasion."

I didn't say anything. If Bessie wants to think she's such a help, let her think so.

"Sometimes your husband has a good day in the business." Bessie went on. "You're not going to make a *gahntze tzimmes* out of it, but still you're happy. And what about when the children bring home good report cards?"

"So you're happy. Where does this fit in a book?"

"How should I know?" said Bessie. "Am I a writer? All I know is that when I brought home a good report, Mama was happy. She would buy me an ice-cream cone. Mama didn't know from child psychology; she just knew that if a child does good it should be rewarded. She knew what to do when a child does bad, too, but that's another story. Look how right she was, to this day I remember . . . a good report, an ice cream."

"Did you do that for your children?"

"What's an ice cream cone today for a child?"

"Then what did you do?"

"I baked a cake," said Bessie, "and on top I would decorate with as many *A*'s as they made on the report. Believe me, for my Joe's *A*'s I didn't need such a big cake, but, thank God, he turned out all right anyway."

"Bessie," I said, "you gave me a good idea. I'll hurry home and write." She didn't really give me an idea, but I wasn't going to sit there and listen to stories about what a great scientist her Joe turned out to be. If he's that great, why doesn't he win the Nobel Prize?

A-TYPE CAKES

Mrs. Joel M. (Shirley) Thrope of Nashville, Tennessee, calls this Banana Nut Loaf her "all-occasion" cake because it goes to bar mitzvahs, weddings, and even Mah-jongg games. Shirley says that the only thing difficult about making this cake is keeping the children from eating the bananas.

BANANA NUT LOAF

¼ c. shortening
¾ c. sugar
2 eggs
1 c. mashed (very ripe) bananas
2 c. sifted flour
2 tsp. baking powder
½ tsp. salt
1 c. chopped walnuts

Cream shortening and sugar well. Add eggs. Continue beating until light. Stir in mashed bananas.

Sift together dry ingredients and add to creamed mixture, beating until smooth. Pour into a greased 9-by-5-by-3 loaf pan. Bake at 350° 60-70 minutes. Cool on cake rack.

An entire football team will vouch for Mrs. Michael Zane's Chocolate Cake. When her daughter was a senior at Hoover High School in Canton, Ohio, Mrs. Zane baked a huge cake (five times the recipe) to represent a football field complete with ball and goal posts. The cake, placed on a large piece of plywood that was decorated with school colors and lighted by huge candles, was carried into the school gym, where a Victory Dance was in full swing. The boys of the team ate the cake the next evening after winning the final game of the season.

CHOCOLATE CAKE

½ c. shortening
1½ c. sugar
2 eggs
1 tsp. vanilla extract
2 oz. unsweetened chocolate, melted
2 c. cake flour
Pinch of salt
1 c. buttermilk
1 tsp. baking soda
1 Tbs. vinegar

Cream together shortening and sugar. Add eggs and vanilla. Add melted chocolate to creamed mixture.

Add salt to flour and add alternately with buttermilk to the creamed mixture. Beat well.

Dissolve soda in vinegar. Stir into batter.

Bake at 350° in two greased and lightly floured 9-inch layer pans, until cake tests done, about 35-40 minutes.

CHOCOLATE FROSTING

5 to 7 Tbs. light cream
3 c. confectioners sugar
3 Tbs. butter
2 oz. unsweetened chocolate
Pinch of salt
1 tsp. vanilla extract

Blend 5 Tbs. cream with sugar (add the remaining cream later, if necessary). Melt the butter and chocolate together. Add to the sugar-cream mixture. Add salt and vanilla. Beat to a spreading consistency.

The recipe for the following chiffon-type cake comes from Rhoda (Mrs. Harry) Nussbaum of Canton, Ohio:

CHOCOLATE SPONGE CAKE

8 eggs, separated
½ c. cold water
1¾ c. sugar
1 c. flour
½ c. cocoa
¾ tsp. cream of tartar
¾ tsp. baking powder
1 tsp. vanilla extract

Beat together egg whites and water until they form soft peaks. Continue to beat while slowly adding sugar. Sift together flour, cocoa, cream of tartar and baking powder 3 times. Fold, a little at a time, into beaten egg whites. Add egg yolks, which have been beaten lightly with the vanilla.

Bake at 350° in an ungreased 10-inch tube pan, until cake tests done, about 45-50 minutes. Invert to cool.

"You know me how I am," said my friend Bessie, "I don't like to throw out. I had a piece of yeast and I was going to make a coffee cake, but my Jake didn't want. So I put the yeast in a chocolate cake. Did it hurt?" I had to admit that it didn't hurt at all. It's an excellent cake with an unusual, but not a yeasty, flavor.

CHOCOLATE CAKE WITH YEAST

1 c. butter or shortening
2 c. sugar
3 eggs, separated
3 oz. unsweetened chocolate, melted
1 c. milk
½ cake yeast
¼ c. lukewarm water
2¾ c. sifted cake flour
½ tsp. salt
1 tsp. baking soda
3 Tbs. hot water
1½ tsp. vanilla extract

Cream butter or shortening. Add sugar slowly, continuing to cream until light and fluffy. Add egg yolks. Beat well. Blend in melted chocolate and milk. Stir in yeast, which has been dissolved in the lukewarm water. Sift together flour and salt. Add to the creamed mixture blending thoroughly. Fold in stiffly beaten egg whites. Cover and refrigerate overnight.

When ready to bake, remove from refrigerator. Batter will look like a block of chocolate ice cream and will be thick enough to slice. Stir in soda, which has been dissolved in hot water. Stir in vanilla. Blend well.

Pour into two greased and lightly floured 9-inch layer pans. Bake at 350° until cake tests done, 40-45 minutes. Ice with your favorite chocolate or mocha icing.

This fudgy chocolate cake contributed by Anna Leah (Mrs. Bert) Blieden of Louisville, Kentucky, can be baked almost before the ink dries on your children's report cards.

QUICK CHOCOLATE CAKE

½ lb. butter
1 c. water
2 c. sugar
2 c. flour
6 Tbs. cocoa
2 eggs
1 tsp. baking soda
½ c. buttermilk*
1 tsp. vanilla extract

In a saucepan, melt butter in water. Bring just to a boil. Remove from flame. Set aside. In a mixing bowl, combine sugar, flour and cocoa. Stir in melted butter. Stir in eggs. Stir baking soda into buttermilk and add to batter. Stir in vanilla. Pour into a greased 13-by-9-by-2⅝ cake pan. Bake at 350° until it tests done, about 30 minutes. Ice while it's still hot.

* If you don't have buttermilk, stir 1 Tbs. lemon juice or vinegar into 1 cup of sweet milk.

ICING

¼ lb. butter
6 Tbs. milk
4 Tbs. cocoa
1 lb. confectioners sugar

In a medium-sized saucepan, melt butter in milk. Remove from flame. Stir in cocoa and sugar. Spread on hot cake.

David Sagerman is as enthusiastic about his cake baking as he is about his hobbies of woodworking, gardening, stamp and coin collecting. He takes pride in finding the easy way to baking success, so you'll find his Date-Nut Loaf no trouble at all.

DATE-NUT LOAF

8 oz. dates, cut up
1½ c. hot water
1 c. sugar
1 Tbs. butter
1 egg
1¼ tsp. baking powder
1¼ tsp. baking soda
½ tsp. salt
2¾ c. flour
1 tsp. vanilla extract
1 c. English walnuts, broken

Add cut-up dates to hot water. Set aside.

Mix together sugar, butter and egg. Stir baking powder, baking soda and salt into flour. Combine flour mixture with sugar-butter-egg mixture. Stir in vanilla.

Add nuts, and date mixture. Stir by hand until the batter is of an even consistency.

Bake in buttered and lightly floured loaf pan 6-by-9¾by-2½ at 350° until it tests done, about 1 hour.

Diane Cohen's Hot Milk Cake will keep for ten days or even longer, but you'll have eaten it up long before then.

HOT MILK CAKE

6 eggs
2 c. sugar
2 c. flour
½ tsp. salt
2 tsp. vanilla extract
2 tsp. baking powder
½ c. boiling milk
¾ c. melted butter
½ c. chopped English walnuts

CRUMB TOPPING

2 Tbs. butter
2 Tbs. sugar
½ tsp. cinnamon

Beat eggs and sugar until thick and lemon-colored. Add flour, salt and vanilla. Mix well.

Sprinkle the baking powder over the batter. Pour the boiling milk and melted butter over the batter (the baking powder will foam up). Fold mixture well.

Grease a 10-inch tube pan. Spread chopped nuts on the bottom. Combine the crumb topping ingredients and spread over the nuts. Pour batter into pan.

Bake at 325° for 1 hour and 20 minutes. Cool. Invert pan over serving dish and remove cake from pan. The crumb mixture will be on top.

15

'C' is for Carrot Cake

If you want a Jewish recipe, go to my friend Irene. She has all her mother's recipes written down on filing cards. Don't think it was easy. It was not like copying recipes—A for *arbes*, B for *bagel*, or c for carrot cake. Her mother had a filing system, it's true, but it was all in her head. Besides, Mama used different measures—a glass of sugar, a half-glass oil, a *schmitzick* salt, a *bissel* baking powder, and a sifter-full flour. It was years before Irene discovered that a glass is equivalent to a standard measuring cup. I don't know how she interpreted *bissel* and *schmitzick*, but since everything Irene makes turns out perfect, I imagine she worked it out correctly.

Irene didn't begin saving these recipes until after she was married. Why should she? If she wanted strudel or *mandel brodt*, all she had to do was ask Mama to bake it for her. After she was married and away from home, she realized what a treasure of recipes she would lose if she didn't get them written down.

Much of Irene's visiting with her mother had to be done by long-distance telephone, and this is how she got many of the recipes. Irene would ask for a recipe and Mama would refer to her mental file.

"Mama," said Irene, during one of their telephone conversations, "how do you make a carrot cake?"

"A carrot cake?" asked Mama. "Why do you want a carrot cake?"

"I don't know why," said Irene. "I just felt like having a carrot cake."

"So if you'll wait," said Mama, "I'll bake right away and I'll mail it to you."

"But I want to bake it myself."

"So why didn't you say you want to learn and would tell you right away, it shouldn't cost so much money on the phone."

"So tell me now."

"So I'll tell you right away," said Mama. "You know, for the carrot cake you make with grated carrots."

"I know, I know."

"Why do you say, 'I know, I know'? If you know already, why do you ask me?"

"I only know about grating the carrots."

"So you grate the carrots. You take a glass oil, a glass carrots, and a glass sugar. Then you put in two eggs and a *bissel* baking powder. You mix together and you bake."

"How long do you bake it?"

"Such a question," said Mama. "You bake till it's done."

"Mama, how hot should I make the oven?"

"The oven should be not too hot and not too cold."

Irene baked the cake. After an hour in a not-too hot, not-too cold oven, the cake was brown around the edges but still soupy in the middle. Irene poured out the cake and called her mother again.

"Mama," she asked, "what did I do wrong?"

Mama reviewed the recipe. "You put in a glass oil, a glass carrots, and a glass sugar?"

Irene assured her that she had.

"You put in two eggs, the baking powder, and the flour?"
"But, Mama," said Irene, "you didn't tell me flour."
"Why should I tell you flour?" said Mama. "Any fool knows that in cake you put in flour."

Here is my friend Irene's recipe for Carrot Cake. Even though any fool knows that in cake you put in flour, Irene isn't taking any chances. She includes the flour in her recipe.

"This is Mama's Carrot Cake," says Irene Conn. "The only change I've made is to substitute the standard measuring cup for the glass. This really isn't necessary, but, who knows, some young cook might use a highball glass."

MAMA'S CARROT CAKE

3 eggs
1 c. sugar
1 c. oil
1 c. grated carrots, firmly packed
2 c. flour
1 tsp. baking soda
1 tsp. baking powder
1 lemon, grated*
1 navel orange, grated*
Orange marmalade or apricot preserves
½ pt. whipping cream

Cream together eggs, sugar and oil. Add the remaining ingredients, except the marmalade and whipping cream. Blend well.

Bake at 350° in two 9-inch layer cake pans which have been greased and lightly floured, until cake tests done, about 30-35 minutes.

When cakes are cool, spread marmalade or preserves between layers. Just before serving, top with whipped cream.

* Irene's mama used to grate the whole lemon and ½ orange on a grater, but you can run them through the fine blade of your food chopper or "grate" in your electric blender at slowest speed.

From the files of Mrs. H. L. Hollander.

CARROT CAKE

1½ c. oil
1¼ c. sugar
4 eggs
3 c. flour
1½ tsp. baking soda
2 tsp. cinnamon
½ tsp. salt
3 c. grated carrots
½ c. chopped pecans
½ c. white raisins (optional)

Mix together oil and sugar. Add eggs, one at a time, beating well after each addition.

Mix together flour, soda, cinnamon and salt. Add to first mixture. Mix at low speed on electric mixer.

Fold in, by hand, carrots, pecans and raisins.

Bake in three lightly greased and floured 9-inch layer pans at 350° until cake tests done, about 50-60 minutes. Glaze while still warm, or cool and frost.

GLAZE

Combine 1 c. confectioners sugar and the juice of 2 lemons. Pour over cakes while still warm.

FROSTING

8 oz. cream cheese
1 lb. confectioners sugar
1 tsp. vanilla extract
½ c. very finely dropped pecans

Cream together cheese and sugar. Add vanilla and pecans. Beat until smooth.

16

Happy Birthday to You

"You're writing a book about happy occasions," my friend Bessie said to me one day, "so why don't you tell people what to do they should enjoy the happy occasion."

"Bessie," I said, "when people have happy occasions they're happy. Otherwise they would be called everyday occasions not to mention, God forbid, sad occasions, which I'm not mentioning in the book."

"Look how you are," said Bessie. "I'm not a writer and I know that people can have happy occasions and be sad because they don't know what to do to enjoy it—like, for instance, Jake's birthday next week."

"So why didn't you tell me it's Jake's birthday? What's to hide?"

"Who's hiding?" said Bessie. "His close friends remember that his birthday comes every year the same time. Why should other people be interested?"

"Now don't call me 'other people,' Bessie. You know I'm your best friend."

"So if you're my friend, you'll tell me what to do to celebrate."

"It's Jake's birthday, so why don't you do what Jake would like to do?"

"This kind of advice I don't need from you," said Bessie. "You know what Jake likes to do. He likes to take a little nap before dinner, to read a little, and to fall asleep watching television. For his birthday I'd like something different."

"Have a surprise dinner party. When he comes home, the house should be dark. Then when he opens the door everybody can shout 'Surprise! Happy birthday!'"

"He'll open the door and people will shout 'Surprise,' so he'll have right away a heart attack and we won't have to worry about what to do for his birthdays any more because this will be the last one."

"So tell him you're making a birthday dinner."

"He'll think I'm crazy making such a fuss over his birthday. He'll say it's foolishness and he don't want."

"I've got a good idea," I said. "Go away for the weekend to that place—you know the one I mean—where they have mineral baths and massage. It'll be a nice rest."

"I'm sick already from resting," said Bessie. "And you know Jake, he'll say the food is better at home. And what kind of pleasure is it to listen to people talk about their diets and their arthritis? Besides, if we go on a weekend, Jake'll miss his regular pinochle game."

"So if you won't go away and you won't have a party, why don't we all go out to a night club? They'll bring in a birthday cake and the orchestra will play 'Happy Birthday, dear Jake' and we'll enjoy like other people seem to enjoy."

"You should know Jake better," said Bessie. "He's a quiet man. The orchestra will play 'Happy Birthday, dear Jake,' he'll run like from a fire."

"That's what you think, Bessie," I said. "Men like attention. Besides, there'll be a good floor show with comics and singing and pretty girls dancing. Maybe he won't let on that he likes it, but he'll like it."

"Wait a minute, wait a minute," said Bessie. "You gave me a good idea."

"So shall I make the reservations? We want to get a good table. What night club should we go to?"

"What night club, when night club?" said Bessie.

"What do you mean, 'What night club, when night club?' I suggested that we go to a club and you said it was a good idea."

"I said you gave me a good idea and you did. You were talking about pretty girls dancing, and pretty girls dancing —showing their legs and God knows what else—is called 'cheesecake,' am I right? And there's nothing that Jake likes better than a good piece of cheesecake. So I'll bake him a cheesecake and I'll see that the pinochle game should be by us and that will be for him a happy birthday. So it shouldn't be a total loss, I'll call some of the girls over and we'll play Mahj."

Well, that's my friend Bessie!

"Easy to make and always a success," says Mrs. Harold (Phyllis) Jacobs, of her favorite Cream Cheese Cake, the recipe of which follows. The walnuts in the crust give it that extra-special flavor that you'll love. Phyllis is an active member of Beth Ahm Sisterhood in Springfield, New Jersey.

CREAM CHEESE CAKE WITH WALNUT CRUST

CRUST

1¼ c. graham cracker crumbs
2 tsp. sugar
2 Tbs. melted butter
¼ c. walnuts, chopped fine

Combine all ingredients. Press into the bottom and half-way up the sides of a greased 8-inch spring form. Bake at 375° for 8 minutes.

FILLING

1 lb. cream cheese
1 c. sugar
3 eggs
1 tsp. vanilla extract
1 pt. commercial sour cream

Beat together the cream cheese and sugar. Blend in eggs. Add vanilla. Fold in sour cream. Pour into graham cracker shell. Bake at 375° for 30 minutes. Turn off heat and leave cake in the oven (with door closed) for an hour.

"It's not what Mama used to make," says Mrs. Seymour (Millie) Alper, of her Cream Cheese Pie, "but it has brought me many compliments." Your guests will love this luscious treat too. Millie, a New Yorker who now makes Wilmington, North Carolina, her home, enjoys giving big parties. If she is serving the Cream Cheese Pie, she quadruples the recipe. Millie thinks it's just as simple as making a single pie.

CREAM CHEESE PIE WITH COINTREAU

CRUST

1¾ c. graham cracker crumbs (17 crackers)
⅔ c. soft butter
2 tsp. sugar

Mix crumbs with sugar and butter. Spread crumbs on bottom and sides of a 9-inch pie pan.

FILLING

9 oz. cream cheese
½ c. sugar
1 Tbs. Cointreau
2 eggs, beaten

Blend together, until smooth, the cream cheese, sugar and Cointreau. Beat eggs thoroughly and blend into cream cheese mixture. Pour into pie shell. Bake at 375° for 20 minutes. Cool for 30 minutes.

TOPPING

1 pt. commercial sour cream
2 Tbs. sugar
1 Tbs. Cointreau
1 can cherry pie filling

Blend the sour cream, sugar and Cointreau well. Pour over cooled pie. Return to oven. Bake at 450° for about 5 to 7 minutes. Remove from oven. Cool, then refrigerate for at least an hour. When the pie is cold and firm, cover it with the prepared cherry pie filling, carefully spooning the filling over the pie. Refrigerate until ready to serve.

"This cheesecake is supposed to be almost identical to the one served at the Brass Rail Restaurants in New York City," says Helen Saul of Dalton, Georgia. "I've tried many cheesecake recipes, but believe this is the best. I love to serve it to special guests."

HELEN SAUL'S CHEESE CAKE

1½ c. Zwieback crumbs (6 oz. pkg.)
¼ lb. butter
6 eggs, separated
1 c. sugar
1 lb. cream cheese
1 pt. sour cream
1 tsp. vanilla extract
2 tsp. lemon juice
½ tsp. salt
¼ tsp. cream of tartar

Prepare the crust by blending the Zwieback crumbs with the butter. Pat the crumb mixture on the bottom and part way up the sides of a 9-inch spring form.

Beat egg yolks, sugar, cream cheese and sour cream in an electric mixer, 15 minutes at medium speed. While beating add vanilla, lemon juice and salt.

Add cream of tartar to egg whites. Beat until stiff. Fold into the cream cheese mixture. Pour into prepared crust.

Bake at 300° for 1 hour. Turn off heat. Let cake remain in closed oven for 30 minutes. Open oven door and let cake stay in oven for another 30 minutes. Refrigerate for several hours before serving. If desired, top with strawberry glaze.

STRAWBERRY GLAZE

1 qt. fresh strawberries
¾ c. sugar
¼ c. cold water
Pinch of salt
1½ Tbs. cornstarch
1 tsp. butter
Red food coloring

Wash and decap strawberries. Crush enough small, uneven-size berries to make 1 cup. Keep remainder of the berries whole. Combine crushed berries, sugar, cold water. salt and cornstarch in a saucepan. Bring to a boil. Boil for 2 minutes, stirring constantly.

Remove from flame. Stir in butter and enough food coloring to tint the desired shade. Cool slightly. Arrange the whole berries on top of cheese cake and spoon glaze onto berries and cake. Chill for at least 12 hours before serving.

The recipe for the following delicious Cottage Cheese Torte comes from Mrs. Henry Rubel of Louisville, Kentucky:

CHEESE TORTE

CRUST

12 to 14 pieces Zwieback
½ c. (scant) butter
½ c. sugar
2 tsp. cinnamon

FILLING

1 qt. creamed cottage cheese (small curd)
8 eggs, separated
2 c. sugar
¾ pt. whipping cream
5 Tbs. flour
Juice and grated rind of 1 lemon

Crush Zwieback to fine crumbs. Combine crumbs with butter, sugar and cinnamon. Press onto the bottom and part way up the sides of a 10-inch spring form. Allow to set a few hours or overnight before putting in filling. Cream together egg yolks, sugar and cottage cheese. Add cream. Blend in flour. Add lemon juice and grated rind. Beat egg whites until stiff. Fold into the cheese mixture. Pour into the crust. Bake at 275° for 1 to 1¼ hours. Test at the end of 1 hour.

"This cake is absolutely luscious," says Selma Jean Simon of Louisville, Kentucky. "Your guests will lose their minds over it. The cream-cheese topping sinks down into the cake, giving it a marbleized appearance and a delectable taste."

CHOCOLATE CHIP CHEESE CAKE

TOPPING

8 oz. cream cheese
1 egg, unbeaten
½ c. sugar
⅛ tsp. salt
6 oz. pkg. chocolate chips

Combine cheese, egg, sugar and salt. Beat until well blended. Stir in chocolate chips. Set aside.

CAKE

1½ c. flour
1 c. sugar
¼ c. cocoa
1 tsp. baking soda
½ tsp. salt
1 c. water
½ c. oil
1 Tbs. vinegar
1 tsp. vanilla extract

Blend together all ingredients (the batter will be rather thin) and pour into an 8-inch-square pan which has been very generously greased. Drop the topping by spoonfuls over the cake, then spread evenly.

Bake at 350° for 50 minutes. Cool. Cut into squares.

Trust Sylvia Hyman to find another short cut. This time it's a delectable Cream Cheese Pie that forms its own crust.

NO-CRUST CREAM CHEESE PIE

1 lb. cream cheese
1 egg
⅔ c. sugar
2 eggs
½ tsp. almond extract

Beat together until smooth the cheese, 1 egg and sugar. Add 2 more eggs and the almond extract. Beat until smooth, about 2-3 minutes.

Pour into a well-greased 9-inch pie pan (this pie forms its own crust). Bake at 350° about 25-30 minutes. Remove from oven when the center of the pie has risen to the level of the edge. Cool for 20 minutes. As the pie cools, the center part shrinks. Fill the center with sour cream topping:

TOPPING

Blend together 1 pt. commercial sour cream, 3 Tbs. Sugar, and 1 tsp. vanilla extract. Cover pie with topping. Return to oven. Bake 10 minutes. Chill before serving.

Another luscious treat from the files of Mrs. H. L. Hollander.

PARTY CHEESECAKE

CRUST

18 pieces of Zwieback (rolled into crumbs)
2 Tbs. sugar
2 Tbs. butter

Blend these ingredients and press into the bottom of a 9-inch spring form.

FILLING

½ c. sugar
2 Tbs. flour
¼ tsp. salt
6 3-oz. pkgs. cream cheese
1 tsp. vanilla extract
4 egg yolks
1 c. light cream
4 egg whites, stiffly beaten

Combine sugar, flour, salt. Add this to the 18 oz. of cream cheese, which has been softened at room temperature. Beat well. Add vanilla. Add egg yolks, one at a time, beating after each addition. Blend in cream. Fold in stiffly beaten egg whites. Pour this mixture over crumbs.

Bake at 325° until set, about 1 hour. Cool.

TOPPING

Blend 1 pt. commercial sour cream, 3 Tbs. sugar, and 1 tsp. vanilla extract. *Do not beat.* Spread over the top of the cooled cheesecake. Return cake to oven. Bake at 375° for 5 minutes. Cool cake completely before removing the sides of the form. Keep refrigerated until ready to serve.

❤ 17 ❤

Be It Never So Humble

"It should never be so humble, there's no place like home," my friend Bessie said to me one morning shortly after her vacation. We were sitting in her kitchen and she was serving me a slice of her fresh-baked coffee cake. "The man who wrote those words knew what he was talking about."

"Bessie," I said, "you sound to me like you didn't enjoy your vacation."

"What was to enjoy?" said Bessie.

"You take a vacation at an expensive resort hotel and that's all you have to say?"

"When you say 'expensive,' you've right," said Bessie. "The only thing free there was the mineral water, and how much mineral water can a person drink?"

"So why did you go to such a place?"

"Why?" said Bessie. "Why does anyone do anything?" Because someone tells them it's the thing to do. I was talking at the Jewish Center to Annette What's-her-name, you know the one I mean, the one who's such a *macher* there. I was telling her that Jake needs a rest, but we don't know where to go, so she tells me about this place. 'You'll love it there,' she says to me. She used to go there, she tells me, and she made so many friends. 'But I don't mean just friends,' she says, 'I mean real *friends*, lifelong FRIENDS! It's been years, and we still correspond.' Well, when a person talks like that, you listen."

"So did you make friends?" I asked.

"I didn't go looking for lifetime friends," said Bessie. "The lifetime friends I've got at home cause me enough trouble."

I didn't say anything. If I would say, "What kind of trouble did I ever cause you?" there would be an argument and I'd never get to hear her story. Some other time, I'll remind her what she said.

"I don't need new lifetime friends," Bessie went on. "I haven't got time to correspond. I don't even write postcards when I'm on vacation because if I would 'wish you were here' I wouldn't be there. Making lifetime friends, that's a job for Annette What's-her-name. For her it's easy. She's a talker and talkers always find listeners. Must be she's also a writer if she's looking for people to correspond with. No, for lifetime friends I don't go hunting, but you spend so much money on a vacation, you want someone, a living person, should at least say to you good morning, should ask you what you're knitting? so you can say, 'I'm knitting for my granddaughter a sweater,' and take out the pictures and show her."

"No one said good morning to you?"

"So if they said good morning—and, to tell the truth, I was the one to say it first—so what did it mean? Nothing. They got off the elevator, it's like they didn't know you anymore. And the dining room," said Bessie, "big it was like Memorial Auditorium. Every meal the maître d' would put you at a different table so you didn't even get to know the waitresses. And always a table for two so you couldn't even say to someone, 'Pass me, please, the salt.'"

"So what did you do?"

"What could we do?" said Bessie. "Golf we don't play, swimming in the pool was for us a little too cold yet. We sat on the verandah and we rocked. We took walks. We came back and sat on the verandah and rocked again. I knitted. I even embroidered on my tablecloth. I don't mean it to be bragging, but you know that when I embroider on my tablecloth here, strangers come up to watch me work on it. Jake was happy. No one bothered him. He sat and read. I said to Jake, 'When you finish with the newspapers, Jake, read *Jews, God and History*.' I read *The Source*. I thought maybe a Jewish couple would walk by and this way they would see we were Jewish, too. Maybe they'd stop and say a word."

"And what did you do in the evenings?"

"In the evenings Jake and I sat in the cardroom and played like a double solitaire. One time a woman did stop to ask me what we were playing. 'We're playing Spite and Malice,' I told her. 'It's a game my daughter learned in college. I'll teach it to you.' But she said she was really looking for a fourth at bridge. So what can I tell you? I don't play bridge."

"Could I have another tiny slice of coffee cake?" I asked.

"Why not?" said Bessie. "Why do I bake if not for my friends. Have some hot coffee with it."

"I'm glad you're home, Bessie," I said, "but I'm sorry your vacation was such a flop."

"Who said it was a flop?" said Bessie. "It wasn't what you call a fun vacation, but it wasn't a flop. To a thinking person," said Bessie, "nothing is a flop. To a thinking person an experience is an experience and you learn from it. I learned, for instance, that you can get as much from a coffee cake as from a vacation."

"Bessie," I said, "you'll forgive me if I don't follow you."

"What's to follow?" said Bessie. "It's really very simple. Why do I need a vacation? If I want to sleep late, I can sleep late at home. Jake doesn't mind once in a while to make his own breakfast. If I'm tired, I've got plenty of time to rest... but this I don't tell Jake. I don't play golf, I don't play bridge. When I go on vacation I like to go where people are friendly, where you can talk to people. So why should I go on vacation? At home people are friendly. If I want company, all I've got to do is bake a coffee cake. I open up the door to the hall and the smell of my fresh coffee cake goes through the whole apartment building. Right away Mrs. Reilly from across the hall comes with the excuse she'd like to borrow a cup of sugar and Lucille Jones from upstairs, she's known me so long she don't need an excuse, she just says she came because she smelled the cake. Lilly Cohen comes from number four, and in my kitchen this morning was already a regular conference of Christians and Jews. We drank coffee and ate cake and we enjoyed. I don't make friends easy, like Annette What's-her-name. People like me should just stay home and bake coffee cakes."

Sometimes I think my friend Bessie is not such a fool, after all.

♥ 18 ♥

Coffee Cakes and Sweet Rolls That Make Lifelong Friends

If you really want to be a proud cook—the envy of your friends—try this traditional Babka. The recipe is Mildred Bernstein's.

BABKA
(*Yeast Coffee Cake*)

1 pkg. dry yeast
¼ c. lukewarm water
¼ lb. butter
1 c. lukewarm milk
1 tsp. salt
4 c. flour
½ c. sugar
¼ tsp. ground mace
2 eggs, well beaten
Melted butter
½ c. sugar, mixed with
1 tsp. cinnamon
½ c. chopped nuts
½ c. white raisins

Dissolve yeast in lukewarm water. Set aside.

Melt butter in lukewarm milk. Add salt. Set aside.

In a large mixing bowl, mix together flour, sugar and mace. Make a well in the center. To the well, add the milk-butter and the dissolved yeast. Add well-beaten eggs. Beat until the dough leaves the sides of the bowl clean. Cover and set aside to rise until double in bulk, 1½ to 2 hours. Beat down. Allow to rise again about 1 hour. After second rising, divide dough in half. On a floured board, roll out half the dough to a rectangle ¼ inch thick. Spread rectangle with melted butter. Sprinkle with half of cinnamon-sugar mix, nuts and raisins. Roll up tightly, as for a jelly roll. Slice in 1-inch slices. Place slices, barely touching, in a well-greased 9-inch tube pan. Repeat process with second half of dough. Add slices to those in pan. Cover and allow to rise to the top of the pan.

Bake at 350° about 35 minutes.

Another gem from the files of Celia Marks.

BASIC SWEET YEAST DOUGH*

½ c. sugar
½ tsp. salt
2 cakes yeast
1 c. lukewarm milk
2 eggs
4 c. flour, measured before sifting
½ c. corn oil

Into a large mixing bowl, put sugar, salt and crumbled yeast cakes. Over this pour lukewarm milk and stir until yeast is dissolved. Beat in eggs, one at a time. Add 2 cups of flour and beat well. Blend in oil. Add remaining 2 cups of flour.

Beat with a wooden spoon for a few minutes, until dough appears smooth. Cover with a cloth. Allow to rise until double in bulk, about an hour. Punch down. Cover and refrigerate for several hours or overnight.

*This basic dough may be used for dinner rolls, sweet rolls or coffee cake. The following recipe is the filling for coffee cake.

COFFEE CAKE FILLING

¼ lb. butter, melted
1⅔ c. brown sugar
1½ tsp. cinnamon
1 c. pecans, chopped (optional)
⅔ c. white raisins

Remove dough from refrigerator. Place on floured surface. Shape into a smooth mound. Divide dough into three equal parts. Roll each part into a rectangle about ¼ inch thick. Spread with melted butter. Mix together brown sugar and cinnamon and sprinkle generously over dough. Sprinkle with raisins and nuts.

Roll up, as for jelly roll, as tightly as possible. Pinch ends of roll to seal. Place on a lightly greased baking tin. Brush with melted butter. Cover. Let rise until doubled in bulk 1½ to 2 hours. Bake at 350° about 25 minutes.

Remove to cooling rack immediately. While cake is still warm (not hot), drizzle icing over it.

ICING

2 Tbs. butter
¾ c. (approx.) confectioners sugar, sifted
1 to 2 Tbs. cream
⅛ tsp. vanilla extract
⅛ tsp. almond extract
Pinch of salt

Melt butter. Add sifted sugar alternately with cream, using only enough cream so that icing will pour. Stir in extracts and salt.

At Louisville bar mitzvahs, everyone looks for Becie's Coffee Cake. Becie is Mrs. Leonard Potash. Her recipe follows.

BECIE'S COFFEE CAKE

1 c. shortening (½ butter)
1½ c. sugar
4 eggs, separated
3 c. flour
3 tsp. baking powder
1 tsp. salt
1¼ c. milk
1 tsp. vanilla extract

STREUSEL TOPPING

Combine ½ cup sugar, 2 tsp. cinnamon, 1 Tbs. cocoa and ½ cup finely chopped nuts. Set aside.

Cream together shortening and sugar. Add egg yolks, one at a time, beating after each addition.

Sift flour. Add baking powder and salt. Sift again. Add flour mixture alternately with milk to creamed mixture. Stir in vanilla. Fold in stiffly beaten egg whites.

Pour ⅓ of the batter into a greased 10-inch tube pan. Sprinkle ⅓ of the streusel over this. Continue the process, ending with streusel. Dot with butter.

Bake at 375° until it tests done, about 60-70 minutes. After about 45 minutes, check to see if streusel topping is browning too quickly. If it is, cover the cake with a piece of brown paper.

An easy-to-make, easy-to-eat Coffee Cake from the files of Mrs. H. L. Hollander.

BLUEBERRY COFFEE CAKE

½ lb. butter
2 c. sugar (or less)*
2 tsp. vanilla extract
4 eggs
2 egg yolks
2 c. flour
1 pkg. (10 oz.) frozen blueberries, defrosted and drained

Cream together butter and sugar thoroughly. Stir in vanilla, eggs and extra egg yolks. Blend well. Fold in flour which has been sifted 4 times. Fold in blueberries. Pour into a greased and lightly floured 9-by-9 cake pan. Bake at 350° about 50 to 60 minutes. Cut into squares when cool.

*If you like it sweet you put in 2 cups of sugar. If you don't like it so sweet, don't put in so much. After all, how should I know how you like your coffee cake? You may say, "Oh, the cake's too sweet," and never bake it again. That would be a shame, when all you have to do is take out a little sugar.

This Coffee Cake takes a lot of doing, but won't you be proud of yourself when you've baked it! It's a favorite with readers of Celia Marks's column.

COFFEE CAKE
(from *The Chattanooga Times*)

PART I

2 cakes yeast
⅓ c. lukewarm water
½ lb. butter
½ c. sugar
3 eggs
2 c. flour
½ tsp. salt
1 c. buttermilk or sour cream
1 tsp. grated lemon rind
2 c. flour
1 tsp. grated orange rind

Dissolve yeast in lukewarm water. Set aside. Cream together butter and sugar. Add eggs, one at a time, beating well after each addition. Sift together 2 cups flour and the salt. Add to creamed mixture. Add dissolved yeast. Mix well. Add buttermilk (or sour cream). Beat well. Stir in lemon rind. Remove cup of batter to a medium-size bowl and set aside. To the batter in the larger bowl, add 2 cups flour and 1 tsp. orange rind. Beat well. Cover with a cloth. Set aside to rise until doubled in bulk, about an hour.

PART II

⅛ lb. butter
½ c. flour, sifted with
1 tsp. cinnamon
¾ c. light brown sugar
1 tsp. grated orange rind
1 c. white raisins
⅔ c. chopped pecans or walnuts

Add the above ingredients to the reserved 1 cup of batter, blending thoroughly. Cover with a cloth and set aside to rise for about an hour. (The smaller portion will not rise as much as the larger.) When both batters have risen, punch them down, cover, and refrigerate until the next day.

The next day, remove the smaller portion of dough from the refrigerator several hours before the larger portion. This will permit it to soften sufficiently.

When ready to bake, turn out larger portion on a well-floured board. Divide in half. Roll each half to a rectangle about 10 inches wide and ⅓ inch thick.

Returning to the smaller, fruited portion, stir it with a wooden spoon to soften. Divide in half. Place small mounds of fruited dough on rolled dough. Using a knife dipped repeatedly in hot water, carefully spread the mounds over the rolled dough. Roll up quickly, as for a jelly roll. Place roll halfway around the bottom of a greased 10-inch tube pan. Repeat with remaining half. Cover pan with a cloth. Place in a warm spot and allow to rise until doubled in bulk, 1½ to 2 hours. Bake at 350° until it tests done, about 45 minutes. Turn out of pan. Turn again to bring top side up. Spread with icing while still warm.

ICING

¾ c. confectioners sugar
¼ tsp. vanilla extract
2 Tbs. butter, melted
Milk

Add sugar and vanilla to melted butter. Add only enough milk to blend to a pouring consistency.

VARIATION: SWEET ROLLS

Follow procedure as in above recipe. When you come to Part II, do not divide dough. Roll out the complete larger portion to ⅓-inch thickness. Spread with softened filling dough. Roll up quickly, as for a jelly roll. Using a sharp knife, cut quickly into ½-inch slices. Place, cut-side down and edges touching, on a greased baking sheet. Cover. Allow to rise until doubled in bulk, about an hour. Bake at 350° for about 25 minutes. Frost.

Carol (Mrs. Edwin) Brooklyn is the young mother of four young children, yet she still finds time to be president of the Cranston (Rhode Island) League of Women Voters and to follow her hobby of "cooking interestingly." This coffee cake is a favorite of hers because it comes closest to the kind her mother used to bake.

COFFEE-BREAK CAKE

½ c. butter	**½ tsp. salt**
1 c. sugar	**2 tsp. baking powder**
1 Tbs. brown sugar	**¾ c. milk**
1 egg	**1 tsp. vanilla extract**
2 c. flour	**¼ tsp. almond extract**

TOPPING

2 Tbs. butter, melted	**¼ tsp. nutmeg**
1½ tsp. cinnamon	**½ c. sugar**

Cream butter thoroughly, add sugars gradually, continuing to beat until light and fluffy. Add egg and beat well.

Sift together dry ingredients and add alternately with milk to the creamed mixture. Add flavorings. Pour into a greased 8-inch-square pan.

Mix topping ingredients together thoroughly. Sprinkle evenly over batter. Bake at 400° for about 25 minutes.

A healthful hint comes from Elizabeth Cohen, along with her favorite coffee-cake recipes. "If you're worried about cholesterol," says she, "use corn-oil margarine for baking, but add commercial butter extract for a rich, buttery flavor."

COFFEE CAKE SUPREME

½ lb. butter or margarine
1 c. sugar
3 eggs
3 c. flour
2½ tsp. baking powder
½ tsp. salt
½ tsp. baking soda
½ pt. commercial sour cream
½ tsp. vanilla extract

Cream together butter and sugar. Add eggs and beat until light and fluffy.

Sift together several times flour, baking powder and salt. Stir baking soda into sour cream. Add flour mixture and soda-sour cream mixture alternately to creamed mixture. Add vanilla. Prepare Streusel.

STREUSEL

¾ c. brown sugar
1 tsp. cinnamon
½ c. chopped nuts

Combine brown sugar, cinnamon and nuts. Sprinkle ⅓ of this streusel on a well-greased and lightly floured 9-inch tube pan. Pour ⅓ of the batter over this. Repeat this process twice. Bake at 350° until it tests done, about 1 hour. Invert pan on cooling rack.

Whenever I drop in to see my friend Bessie, she serves me coffee with these sweet rolls. Sometimes I say to her, "Bessie, how come you always have these rolls? You must have baked a million of them." Bessie says, "What's the matter, you don't like them? You don't have to eat them." My friend Bessie is that touchy. She ought to know by now that that's why I drop in so often.

COTTAGE CHEESE SWEET ROLLS

½ c. butter
1 c. cottage cheese
2 c. flour
1 rounded tsp. baking powder
Pinch of salt
Your favorite preserves
1 egg yolk
Confectioners sugar

Into a large mixing bowl, put butter, cheese, flour, baking powder and salt. Knead to a dough. Cover the bowl and let the dough rest for an hour. On a lightly floured pastry board, roll out dough to ¼-inch thickness. Cut into 3-inch squares. Place a teaspoon of preserves in the center of each square. Fold squares to form triangles, pinching edges together tightly to seal. Brush with beaten egg yolk. Bake at 350° until golden brown, about 18-20 minutes. Remove to platter. Dust with confectioners sugar. Makes about 20.

The following recipe for a light, luscious, and easy-to-make coffee cake comes from Mrs. David A. (Annette) Sagerman of Louisville, Kentucky. If your husband, brother, or son saw military service at Fort Knox, he will remember "Mrs. USO." Annette can never enjoy a Jewish holiday until every one of "her" soldiers has been offered home hospitality.

CREAM CHEESE COFFEE CAKE

¼ lb. butter
½ lb. cream cheese
1¼ c. sugar
2 eggs
2 cups flour
1 tsp. baking powder
½ tsp. baking soda
1 tsp. vanilla extract
¼ tsp. salt
¼ c. milk

TOPPING

⅓ c. brown sugar
2 Tbs. butter
⅓ c. flour
½ tsp. cinnamon

Cream butter and cheese. Gradually add sugar, continuing to beat. Add eggs, one at a time, beating after each addition. Stir in vanilla. Sift together flour, baking powder, soda and salt. Add to creamed mixture alternately with milk. Spread in a greased 9-by-13-by-2⅝ cake pan. Combine topping ingredients into a crumbly mixture. Sprinkle evenly over the top of the batter. Bake at 350° about 35-40 minutes. Cut into squares when cool.

Another recipe from the Queen of Coffee Cake Bakers—Celia Marks.

CRUMB-FILLED COFFEE CAKE

1 cake yeast
¾ c. lukewarm milk
2 c. flour
6 Tbs. sugar
½ tsp. salt
¾ c. butter
1 egg, beaten (reserve 1 Tbs. for brushing tops)
½ tsp. grated orange rind
1½ c. flour

Dissolve yeast in lukewarm milk. Sift 2 cups of flour into a large mixing bowl. Stir in sugar and salt. Cut in butter until particles are fine. Add beaten egg and orange rind. Add yeast-milk mixture. Mix thoroughly. Work in remaining 1½ cups flour to form a stiff dough.

On a floured surface, knead until smooth and satiny (about 3 minutes). Place in bowl. Cover with a cloth. Set in a warm place. Allow to rise for about 1 hour. While dough is rising, prepare filling and topping.

FILLING

1⅓ c. sweet crumbs (stale cake, macaroons, or any crisp cookies, crushed)
¼ c. sugar
1 tsp. cinnamon
½ c. melted butter
1 c. white raisins
½ c. chopped nuts

Combine all ingredients in order given.

TOPPING

Reserved 1 Tbs. egg
1 Tbs. water
¼ c. sugar
¼ c. nuts, finely chopped

When ready to bake, divide dough in half. On a floured surface, roll out half of dough to a rectangle 6-by-18 inches. Spread half of the filling lengthwise, down the center of the rectangle. Fold the sides of the rectangle to meet in the center. Seal with fingers. Seal the ends of the strip. Repeat with remainder of dough. Shape into crescents. Place on a lightly greased baking sheet. Cover with cloth and leave at room temperature for 1 hour. Blend the reserved 1 Tbs. of egg with 1 Tbs. water. Brush this on top of the cakes. Sprinkle with a mixture of ¼ cup sugar and ¼ cup finely chopped nuts. Bake at 350° about 25-30 minutes.

Here's a coffee cake you'll be proud to serve. The recipe that follows comes from Mrs. Samuel Reinglass:

FORM COFFEE CAKE

1 c. milk
1 cake yeast
⅛ tsp. salt
2 c. flour
¼ lb. butter
1 c. sugar
3 eggs
Rind of 1 lemon, grated
Juice of ½ lemon
⅛ tsp. grated nutmeg
1¼ to 1½ c. flour
½ c. currants
½ c. chopped nuts

Scald milk and cool to lukewarm (105-115°). Pour milk into a large mixing bowl. Crumble yeast into milk and allow to soften. Add salt and 2 cups of flour. Beat until smooth. Let rise in a warm place until doubled in bulk, about an hour.

Cream together thoroughly butter and sugar. Add eggs, one at a time, beating well after each addition. Stir in lemon rind, juice, and nutmeg.

Mix this batter with the yeast batter, which has now doubled in bulk. Beat well. Add enough flour to make a thick batter. Beat until smooth. Stir in currants and nuts. Pour into a greased 10-inch tube pan or *Kugelhof,* filling pan ½ full. Let rise in a warm place until pan is almost full, about an hour. Bake at 375° for 10 minutes. Reduce heat to 350° and continue to bake until it tests done, about 35-45 minutes. Remove from pan. Ice with Confectioners Icing while still warm.

CONFECTIONERS ICING

2 Tbs. melted butter
¾ c. (approx. confectioners sugar
1 to 2 Tbs. cream
Pinch of salt
⅛ tsp. almond extract
⅛ tsp. vanilla extract

Add sifted sugar alternately with cream to the melted butter, using only enough sugar so that icing will pour. Stir in salt and extracts.

Here's another delicious coffee cake from Elizabeth Cohen.

FRENCH COFFEE CAKE

3 c. flour
4 tsp. baking powder
½ tsp. salt
2 c. sugar
½ lb. butter
4 eggs
1 can (14 oz.) evaporated milk
1 tsp. vanilla extract
1 tsp. lemon juice
½ tsp. grated lemon rind
¼ c. cinnamon-sugar mix
½ c. chopped nuts

Sift together flour, baking powder, salt and sugar. Add butter and crumble. *Reserve ½ cup* of this crumble mixture. To the remainder of the crumble add eggs, milk, flavorings and lemon rind. Blend well. Put half of this batter into a greased and lightly floured 10-inch tube pan. Sprinkle with cinnamon-sugar mix and nuts. Add remaining batter. Cover with reserved ½ cup of crumbs. Bake at 375° until it tests done, about 1 hour.

Another Chattanooga favorite is this French Coffee Cake from the files of Celia Marks.

FRENCH COFFEE CAKE

1 cake yeast
¼ c. lukewarm water
4 c. flour
¼ c. sugar
1 tsp. salt
½ lb. butter
1 c. lukewarm milk
3 egg yolks, beaten

FILLING

3 egg whites, beaten
1 c. sugar
2 tsp. cinnamon
1 c. chopped nuts
1 c. white raisins

Dissolve yeast in lukewarm water. Set aside. Into a large mixing bowl, sift together flour, sugar and salt. Cut in butter with a pastry blender until it is the size of small peas. Add warm milk, beaten egg yolks and dissolved yeast. Beat well for a few minutes. Cover bowl with a cloth. Refrigerate overnight. When ready to bake, divide dough into two parts. Roll each half on a floured board to a rectangle ¼-inch thick. Spread dough with stiffly beaten egg whites. Combine sugar, cinnamon, nuts and raisins. Sprinkle over egg white. Roll up dough as for a jelly roll. Place in two greased loaf pans. Cover. Let rise until doubled in bulk, about an hour. Bake at 350° for about 45 minutes. Frost while still warm.

FROSTING

¾ c. confectioners sugar
1 to 2 Tbs. milk
¼ tsp. almond extract

Combine all ingredients, adding just enough milk to make of pouring consistency.

Diane (Mrs. Jules) Cohen of East Greenwich, Rhode Island, loves to cook and bake for her husband and three young children, and for neighbors and friends. This French Coffee Cake is one of her favorites.

FRENCH COFFEE CAKE

½ lb. butter or margarine
1 c. sugar
3 eggs
1 c. commercial sour cream
2¼ c. flour
1 tsp. baking powder
1 tsp. baking soda
1 tsp. vanilla extract

TOPPING

⅔ c. brown sugar
2 Tbs. butter
3 Tbs. flour
1 tsp. cinnamon

Cream together butter and sugar. Add eggs one at a time, beating after each addition. Blend in sour cream. Sift flour, baking powder and baking soda into the creamed mixture. Add vanilla. Mix well and pour into a well-greased or paper-lined 9-inch square pan. Mix topping ingredients together and sprinkle over batter. Bake at 350° for about 35 minutes.

An easy-to-make, easy-to-eat coffee cake is this one from Cousin Reva, Mrs. James Kasdan of Louisville, Kentucky.

MAMA ANNIE'S COFFEE CAKE

2 c. flour
2 tsp. baking powder
1 c. sugar
¼ lb. butter
2 eggs
½ c. milk
½ tsp. vanilla extract

Sift together flour, baking powder and sugar. Cut in butter until the texture is that of coarse meal. Reserve ½ cup of this mixture for topping. To the remainder add eggs, milk and vanilla. Beat until smooth. Pour into a greased 9-by-9 pan. Top with the following:

TOPPING

½ c. reserved mixture
1 Tbs. butter
¼ c. brown sugar (firmly packed)
1 tsp. cinnamon
¼ tsp. nutmeg
¼ c. raisins, dusted with flour (optional)

Mix together all ingredients and spread over batter. Bake at 350° for 30 minutes. Cut into squares when cool.

Lillian (Mrs. Max L.) White of Providence, Rhode Island, is a homemaker who loves to cook. She also likes to sing, and her Meringue Coffee Cake is something to sing about! Her recipe follows:

MERINGUE COFFEE CAKE

2 cakes compressed yeast
½ c. lukewarm milk
½ lb. butter
¼ c. sugar
3 egg yolks (reserve whites)
½ tsp. vanilla extract
4 c. flour, sifted
½ c. sour cream
1 c. sugar
2 Tbs. cinnamon
½ c. chopped nuts
½ c. raisins

Dissolve yeast in lukewarm milk. Cream together butter and ¼ cup sugar. Add egg yolks and vanilla. Mix well.

Add sifted flour alternately with yeast mixture and sour cream. Cover with a towel and refrigerate overnight.

The next morning, beat reserved egg whites. Gradually add 1 cup sugar, continuing to beat until stiff.

On a floured board, roll out dough to a rectangle 12 by 15 inches. Spread with meringue. Sprinkle meringue with cinnamon, nuts and raisins. Roll up as a jelly roll. Cut into 6 equal parts. Place, cut side down, in the bottom of a greased 10-inch tube pan. Meringue filling will be oozing out of slices. Cover with a towel and let rise for 2 hours.

Bake at 350° for 1 hour. Cool slightly before removing from pan.

If you want to impress your friends with a beautiful and tasty coffee cake, try this recipe, which comes from Mrs. Charles (Marian) Weisberg of Louisville, Kentucky.

PULL-APART COFFEE CAKE

2 cakes yeast
½ c. sugar
½ lb. butter
3 eggs
5½ c. flour
1 tsp. salt
1 can (6 oz.) evaporated milk with enough plain milk to make 1 cup

FILLING

½ c. white raisins
¼ lb. butter
1 c. brown sugar
2 Tbs. cinnamon
1 c. chopped nuts

Crumble yeast on top of sugar. Set aside until yeast dissolves. It may be necessary to stir yeast through sugar to hasten the process. Cream butter. Add eggs, one at a time, beating after each addition. Add the yeast mixture. Sift together flour and salt and add to batter alternately with milk. Place dough in a greased bowl. Cover with a damp cloth and refrigerate overnight.

When ready to bake, remove dough from refrigerator and let stand at room temperature for about half an hour. Assemble filling ingredients: A bowl of raisins, a bowl of melted butter, and a bowl of brown sugar mixed with cinnamon and nuts.

Pinch off a piece of dough (about the size of a walnut); put a few raisins in it and roll into a ball. Dip ball in melted butter, then in sugar mixture. Place balls in a lightly greased and floured 10-inch tube pan. Continue the process until all the dough has been used. If there is any melted butter left, dribble it over the cake.

Bake at 350° until done, about 1 hour. Remove from pan while still warm, but not hot.

"This Sour Cream Coffee Cake makes a really great dessert," says Mrs. Raphael (Maxine) Hoffman of Wilmette, Illinois. "The best thing about it is that it never fails to come out good!"

SOUR CREAM COFFEE CAKE

¼ lb. butter
1 c. sugar
2 eggs
½ pt. commercial sour cream
2 c. sifted cake flour
1 tsp. baking powder
1 tsp. baking soda
1 tsp. vanilla extract

Cream together butter and sugar. Add eggs and sour cream. Beat until smooth.

Sift together flour, baking powder and baking soda. Add to the creamed mixture. Add vanilla. Blend well.

TOPPING AND FILLING

¼ to ½ c. sugar
3 tsp. cinnamon
½ c. chopped nuts

Combine ingredients. Sprinkle half of this topping on the bottom of a very-well-greased 9-inch tube pan. Pour half of the batter over the topping. Sprinkle remaining topping over batter. Add remaining batter. If desired, run a knife through the batter for marbled effect. Bake at 350° for 35 minutes.

The following Streusel Coffee Cake is such a favorite with her family that Mrs. Eugene (Margaret) Michel of Louisville, Kentucky, baked it for her son's wedding reception:

STREUSEL COFFEE CAKE

½ lb. butter
1½ c. sugar
4 eggs
2 c. flour
1 tsp. baking powder
½ c. milk
1 Tbs. vanilla extract

Cream together butter and sugar for 10 minutes. Add eggs, one at a time, beating after each addition.

Combine flour and baking powder, add to creamed mixture alternately with milk. Add vanilla. Pour into a greased and lightly floured 10-inch spring form. Cover with streusel topping.

TOPPING *

4 Tbs. butter	**4 Tbs. sugar**
1 Tbs. flour	**2 tsp. cinnamon**

Combine all ingredients and sprinkle over the top of the batter.

Bake at 350° until it tests done, about 40-50 minutes.

* The streusel topping sinks down through the cake, some of it ending up on the bottom of the pan. If you're going to remove the cake from the pan, or, rather, the pan from the cake (since it's a spring form), do so while the cake is still slightly warm; otherwise the streusel hardens on the pan.

Another fine recipe from the files of Edna Shaw.

MOTHER'S VIENNESE KUGELHOF

2 cakes yeast	**Juice of 1 lemon**
2 tsp. sugar	**Grated rind of 1 orange**
1 Tbs. flour	**¼ tsp. salt**
2 c. (scant) lukewarm milk	**1½ tsp. vanilla extract**
½ lb. butter	**6 rounded c. (approx.) flour**
4 egg yolks	**1 c. white raisins**
1 c. sugar	**Pecan halves**

Crumble yeast and mix with 2 tsp. sugar and 1 Tbs. flour. Dissolve in 2 Tbs. lukewarm milk. Set aside.

Cream butter. Alternately add egg yolks (one at a time) and sugar, continuing to beat. Add lemon juice, orange rind, salt and vanilla. Beat until smooth.

Alternately add flour and remainder of milk to the creamed mixture, until about ¾ of the flour has been used. At this point, add dissolved yeast. Continue adding flour and milk. If the dough is dry enough to handle, it may not be necessary to add the entire amount of flour. Add raisins.

Beat thoroughly so that all the air is beaten out of the batter. Do not stir, but beat toward yourself until batter leaves the spoon and is smooth. You cannot overbeat. The more you beat, the better the result.

Dust dough with a little flour. Cover the bowl with a cloth. Allow to rise in a warm place until more than double in bulk, about an hour. If not ready to use, punch it down once and let it rise again.

Liberally grease two 9-inch *Kugelhofs* or *Bundt* pans. Dust liberally with flour. Dot pecan halves around the *Kugelhof* form and pour dough in until half full. Allow to rise to double in bulk. Bake at 350° for about 45-55 minutes.

Celia Marks's Pinwheel Rolls will brighten up your Sunday brunch.

PINWHEEL ROLLS

1 c. light cream
½ c. sugar
1 cake yeast
1 c. butter
5 egg yolks
3 c. flour
½ c. sugar (for rolling out dough)
1 c. chopped walnuts, pecans or slivered almonds

Scald cream and cool to lukewarm. Add ½ cup sugar and crumbled yeast cake. Stir until dissolved.

Cream butter until light and fluffy. Add egg yolks, one at a time, beating after each addition.

Sift flour and add alternately with yeast mixture to creamed mixture. Beat thoroughly. Chill overnight.

When ready to bake, mix ½ cup sugar with the chopped nuts. Spread half of this mixture evenly on a large board or rolling surface. Divide dough in half. Using a floured rolling pin, roll dough directly onto sugar-nuts, making sure that all are taken in by the dough. Roll out to ⅛ -inch thickness. Roll up tightly as for a jelly roll. Cut into ½-inch slices. Place 1½ inches apart on a greased baking sheet. Let rise until light, about 1 hour.

Bake at 350° until delicately brown, about 15-20 minutes. Repeat with remaining half of dough. Yield: 3 to 4 dozen small rolls.

From Mrs. Joseph Stern of Roanoke, Virginia, comes this recipe for Schnecken that will brighten up a Sunday brunch or be a tasty treat for any happy occasion.

SCHNECKEN

¼ lb. butter
1 Tbs. sugar
1 egg
2 c. flour
2 tsp. baking powder
½ c. milk (or less)

FILLING

¾ lb. (approx.) butter, melted
1 c. brown sugar
¼ c. granulated sugar
1 Tbs. cinnamon
1 c. raisins
1 c. chopped pecans
½ c. pecan halves

Cream ¼ lb. butter with 1 Tbs. sugar. Add egg. Beat well.

Mix flour with baking powder and add to creamed mixture with enough milk to form a soft dough. Divide the dough in half.

On a lightly floured board, roll out half the dough to a 12-by-12 square. Brush with melted butter. Combine the brown and granulated sugars, cinnamon, raisins and 1 cup chopped pecans. Sprinkle half of this mixture over the dough. Roll up tightly as for jelly roll. Cut in 1-inch slices. Repeat this process with the remaining half of the dough.

Place 1 Tbs. melted butter, 2 tsp. brown sugar and a pecan half in each cup of a muffin tin. Place Schnecken, cut side down, in muffin cups.

Bake at 350° until lightly brown, about 20-25 minutes. Turn out on platter. Glaze with extra syrup in bottom of tins. Makes 24.

Edna Shaw's Viennese Schnecken are superb! They take some effort, but the result makes it all worthwhile. Besides, this recipe makes so many tiny Schnecken that you can freeze them and have them on hand when any party occasion arises.

VIENNESE SCHNECKEN

2 cakes yeast
2 tsp. sugar
2 c. lukewarm milk
½ lb. butter
1 c. sugar
3 egg yolks
1 whole egg
½ tsp. vanilla extract
½ tsp. lemon extract
7 c. flour
1 c. white raisins, washed and well drained

Dissolve yeast and 2 teaspoons sugar in lukewarm milk and set aside.

Cream butter. Gradually add sugar, and cream thoroughly. Beat in egg yolks and whole egg. Add extracts.

Add flour alternately with yeast-milk mixture. (If you are using an electric mixer, the last cup of flour may have to be added by hand.) Beat well with a wooden spoon until blisters form on the dough. Cover with a cloth. Set in warm place to rise until double in bulk, about an hour. While dough is rising, prepare filling.

FILLING

2 c. ground pecans
½ c. brown sugar
½ c. granulated sugar
2 tsp. cinnamon
1 c. strawberry preserves
4 Tbs. orange juice
2 Tbs. lemon juice
2 tsp. grated orange rind
1 tsp. grated lemon rind
1 c. cake or cookie crumbs

FOR MUFFIN TINS

½ lb. butter (approx.) melted
1½ c. brown sugar mixed with
1½ tsp. cinnamon
60 pecan halves
Maple syrup

Prepare the filling by mixing all ingredients together thoroughly. The filling should be firm enough so that none will pour off the side of a spoon. If it is not firm enough, add a bit more cookie crumbs.

Prepare the muffin tins (tiny ones—¾ inch deep, 1¾ inches across the top) by greasing. Place 1 tsp. melted butter, 1 tsp. brown-sugar-cinnamon mix, 1 pecan half, and 1 tsp. maple syrup in each muffin cup. If you like a richer Schnecken, you may put more of each item in the cup.

On a floured board, roll out ⅓ of the dough at a time, to a rectangle, 10-by-20 inches. Spread with melted butter and ⅓ of the Schnecken filling. Roll up tightly as for a jelly roll. Using a sharp knife and quick strokes, cut roll into 1-inch slices. Place slices, cut side down, in prepared muffin tins.

Cover with a cloth. Allow to rise until double in bulk, about an hour.

Bake at 350° for 15 minutes. Remove from tins immediately by inverting on cooling rack. Spoon any remaining syrup from the pans over the Schnecken.

❤ 19 ❤

Strudel and Other Traditional Meicholim

"You're always asking for my strudel recipe," my friend Bessie said to me one day, "so come over to the house tomorrow and you'll watch me how I make it."

Bessie's strudel is just about the best I've ever eaten. The pastry is thin as a piece of tissue paper, and Bessie spreads the filling all over the pastry, not like some strudel where the filling is just in the center. You bite down into a layer of pastry, a layer of filling, a layer of pastry, a layer of filling, and all of it melts in your mouth. Naturally, I wanted Bessie's recipe, but she knows very well that I know how to make strudel, and that all she would have to do is give me a list of the ingredients. I'm not a young bride that I have to watch how she makes it. Of course, I didn't tell her this because my friend Bessie is very touchy; but on the other hand, I didn't want her to think that she was doing me a favor, so all I said was, "What's the occasion?"

Ordinarily, Bessie would have answered my question with another question like, "Does there have to be an occasion?" But Bessie knows that I know that you don't make strudel every day. In the first place, it's a lot of work. In the second place, with all the wonderful things that go into it, who can afford to make it every day? And in the third place, even if you don't mind the work and you can afford it, it's not a way to live. If you ate strudel every day, what would you have to look forward to? You've got to dream about having strudel weeks beforehand, and you've got to remember it weeks after.

"The occasion is," said Bessie, "I'm baking for the wedding. I'll bake now and put in the freezer."

"You're not having the wedding catered?"

"Of course, we'll have it catered, but how can I let my Ruthie, my youngest, get married without a piece of her mama's strudel? My mama baked it for my wedding and her mama baked it for hers. It wouldn't be a wedding without strudel. You'll come to the house, we'll bake the strudel and we'll have a piece with coffee, warm from the oven."

I could see that Bessie wanted someone to talk to, because Bessie doesn't drink coffee in the afternoon unless she's got something on her mind to think about, and when Bessie thinks, she talks, and when she talks, she wants someone to listen. What's a friend for if not to listen? I told her I'd be happy to help her.

When I came to Bessie's the next day, she had already prepared the dough.

"I thought you were going to teach me how to make it," I said, "and you've already mixed the dough."

"What are you, a new bride, that I have to teach you? I'll tell you what goes in it and you'll know."

I copied down the list of ingredients. "This is very much like my mama's strudel," I said, "only you use more oil. Mama put apples and pecans in hers and you're using dates and walnuts."

"Did you come here for your mama's recipe or for my mama's?" I kept quiet.

"Mama used to mix the dough right on the pastry board," Bessie explained. "She put the flour down, then she made a hole in the center and put in the eggs and oil and mixed it all together. I can't do that. I have to use a bowl. Maybe if I had made it at home I would know how, but I didn't make strudel until after I was married. As a matter of fact," said Bessie, "I don't even think I ate a perfect piece of strudel until I was married. At home I didn't get the best pieces; they were saved for company. I ate the end pieces that got a little burned because they were thinner. After I got married, I guess I was company because Mama brought me the fat middle pieces that didn't burn. You know what? I still like the burned pieces."

"Reminiscing," I said, "is reminiscing, and strudel-making is strudel-making. Let me chop the nuts for you."

"Strudel-making *is* reminiscing," said Bessie, "and who chops nuts? I put already everything through the food grinder, the nuts, the dates, the orange, the toast."

"So why did you ask me to help you?"

"Who asked you to help?" said Bessie. "If I'm taking up your valuable time, you'll excuse me, please. I just thought it would be more sociable. While I'm stretching the dough, you can talk to me."

What Bessie really meant was that I could listen to her. All the time she was putting a clean white cloth on the kitchen table and stretching the dough until it was paper-thin and covered the whole table, she was talking. I was watching Bessie with both eyes because nobody can stretch a strudel dough as thin as she can, but I was listening with only one ear because what Bessie has to say I've heard already many times. However, when she said, "You can't tell young people anything these days," I opened up the other ear because I had a feeling that, finally, Bessie was getting to what was really bothering her.

"There was a time when children listened to their parents," Bessie said, "but not now."

"I don't know what you're complaining about," I said. "You have fine children."

"Did I say they weren't fine?" said Bessie.

"Then why are you complaining?"

"Who's complaining?" said Bessie. "All I said is that children don't listen to their parents anymore. A child comes to you and says, 'Mama, I'm going to marry David, so can you tell her 'wait awhile'? Will she listen to you?"

"Did you listen to your mother?"

"What do you mean," said Bessie. "Of course, I did."

"She didn't tell you that you were too young?"

"To tell you the truth, I wasn't so young anymore."

"How did that happen? The way you always tell it, you were the most popular girl. How come you weren't so young when you married Jake?"

"Maybe I wasn't really in love with the other boys. Maybe I just thought I was. With Irv, I was sure it was true love."

"So what was the matter? Didn't your mama like him?"

"Mama was crazy about Irv," said Bessie. "I remember the first time he came to the house. Mama said what a fine boy he was. Only one thing bothered her. She used to worry that his head wasn't shaped good. She said it came to a point."

"So?"

"What do you mean 'so?'" said Bessie. "Would you marry a boy whose head came to a point? I could see that Mama was right. The more I went out with Irv, the more I worried about his head."

"Was he the only one?"

"Do you think I was a wallflower? I had plenty of chances. There was Murray. Mama liked Murray, too. She said he would be perfect except for his chin. She said it was a shame that such a nice boy shouldn't have a chin. Mama was a very observant person. You know, I wouldn't have noticed about his chin if she hadn't pointed it out to me."

"What about Leon Bershoff? You told me once that you were practically engaged to him."

"He talked through his nose," said Bessie. "It irritated me as much as it did Mama."

"It didn't keep him from being an excellent lawyer."

"What am I, on trial?" said Bessie. "Can I help it if I'm sensitive to the way people talk? Mama was the same way."

"So what was with Jake? He must have been perfect?"

"No one is perfect," said Bessie. "Mama used to worry that such a nice boy should be so homely. 'Mama,' I said to her, 'he's as ugly as sin, but I love him.' After that it didn't worry her anymore."

"So why don't you tell your Ruthie that David's head comes to a point, that he has no chin, or that he talks through his nose?"

"Are you crazy?" said Bessie. "David has a beautiful head and with his face he could be in the movies. He's a fine boy and they love each other."

"Then what are you complaining about?"

"Who's complaining?" said Bessie. "Why do you always try to start an argument? You'll make me burn the strudel, and not just the end pieces."

Well, that's my friend Bessie!

BESSIE'S STRUDEL

5 c. flour
¼ c. sugar
Pinch of salt
3 eggs, beaten
¾ c. oil
1 c. lukewarm water

Sift together flour, sugar and salt. Add eggs, oil and water. Mix thoroughly. Cover with a tea towel and let stand while preparing filling.

FILLING

4 c. walnuts
2 pounds pitted dates
3 whole oranges
Rind of 2 lemons
3 or 4 slices crisp toast
1 c. pineapple preserves
1 c. cherry preserves
1 c. plum preserves
2 No. 2 cans crushed pineapple, drained
Oil
2 c. shredded coconut
Cinnamon-sugar mix (1 Tbs. cinnamon, 1 c. sugar)

Put nuts, dates, oranges, and lemon rind through the food grinder. Put enough crisp toast through the grinder to absorb the juices. Mix together the preserves and pineapple.

Knead dough for about 5 minutes on a lightly floured board or a white tablecloth stretched over kitchen table. Divide dough into four parts. Work with one part, keeping remainder in covered bowl.

Roll and stretch the dough to paper thinness. Brush the sheet of dough with oil. Spread with mixed preserves and sprinkle with shredded coconut. Spread with the ground fruit mixture.

Roll up carefully (as for jelly roll) three or four times, and cut from sheet. Continue this process until all the dough has been used.

Brush the top of each roll with oil and sprinkle with cinnamon-sugar mix. Cut diagonally at 1½-inch intervals. Place on liberally oiled shallow baking tins and bake at 350° until lightly browned, about 45 minutes.

My friend Bessie says that her doctor told her that cottage cheese is very healthy. Since she doesn't like to eat it plain, Bessie uses it in pastry whenever she can.

COTTAGE CHEESE STRUDEL

1¼ lb. butter
1 lb. cottage cheese
5 c. flour
Confectioners sugar

Cream together butter and cottage cheese. Blend in flour. Cover bowl and refrigerate overnight.

When ready to bake, divide dough into 6 portions. Work with one portion at a time, keeping remainder refrigerated. Roll out on wax paper that has been liberally dusted with confectioners sugar. Roll out as thin as possible.

Spread with filling (below). Roll up as for a jelly roll. This dough is very fragile and may be difficult to roll up. An easy way to do it is to lift the wax paper slowly and the dough will roll itself. Score lightly at 1½-inch intervals. Bake on an ungreased cookie sheet at 350° until light brown, 25-35 minutes. Cool. Cut into 1½-inch slices. Dust with confectioners sugar.

SUGGESTED FILLINGS

1. apricot preserves, shredded coconut and chopped nuts.
2. plum preserves, shredded apples, raisins and cinamon-sugar mix.
3. brown sugar, cinnamon and chopped nuts.

"My mother created this strudel recipe," says Mrs. Marvin (Ruthie Faye) Waldman, who comes from a family of well-known Louisville, Kentucky, bakers. "Perhaps I should continue to keep it a family secret by leaving out one or two important ingredients as some cooks have been known to do, but I'm so proud of it, why shouldn't everyone enjoy?" Ruthie Faye, the mother of five, keeps young and slim by dancing with the modern dance group of the Jewish Community Center.

STRUDEL À LA SADIE

FILLING

5 Tbs. cherry preserves
5 Tbs. damson plum preserves
5 Tbs. crushed pineapple, drained
1 c. shredded coconut
1 c. nuts, chopped
10 pitted dates, cut up
1 lemon rind, ground
½ orange rind, ground

Combine all ingredients and set aside.

DOUGH

2 c. sifted flour
Pinch of salt
Pinch of baking soda
1½ Tbs. sugar
⅓ c. oil
1 egg, beaten
¼ c. warm water
Cinnamon-sugar mix

Into a mixing bowl, sift together sifted flour, salt, baking soda and sugar. Make a well.

Into the well add oil, egg and warm water. Blend to a dough. Knead. Dough should leave sides of bowl and hands clean. If necessary, add a little more flour. Form into a ball. Divide ball into two or three parts, depending upon how skilled you are at stretching dough. Work with one part, keeping the remainder covered.

On a floured board, roll, stretch, tug, pull, twirl like a pizza, if you can (anything's fair with strudel) to a paper-thin rectangle. The size of the rectangle will depend upon your skill. The dough may tear in spots, but mend the tear and continue stretching. You may eventually become as skilled in stretching dough as was your mother or grandmother. By that time, you may not be able to afford strudel because with that much dough, who can afford the extra filling? Make the rectangle two or three times longer than it is wide.

Starting about 1½ inches from the edge of the dough, place a line of filling lengthwise. Use ⅓ of the filling if you've divided the dough into thirds.

Now, place the clear edge of the dough over the filling and roll up as for a jelly roll. Now very carefully, lift the roll on to a 15-by-10½-by-½ cookie pan which has been liberally oiled (about ¼ inch of oil standing in the pan).

This is a good opportunity to stretch the roll further . . . Pull at both ends as you're setting it down. Brush the roll with oil and sprinkle with cinnamon-sugar mix.

Bake at 350° until delicately browned, 45-50 minutes.

Using a spatula (you shouldn't burn the hands), immediately remove rolls from pan to absorbent paper. Using a very sharp knife, carefully slice the rolls diagonally at 1½ inch intervals. When ready to serve, dust with confectioners sugar. If you don't, the sugarplum fairy at the bar mitzvah is sure to do it, thinking you didn't know any better.

Mrs. David (Hilda) Bordorf has lately turned her talents to arts and crafts. Her *objets d'art* may be found in Louisville decorator shops. It takes the unusual, like this Ice Cream Strudel, to get Hilda back into the kitchen.

ICE CREAM STRUDEL

½ lb. butter
2 c. flour
1 c. vanilla ice cream, melted
1 scant cup apricot preserves
½ c. white raisins
1 c. nuts, finely chopped

Cut butter into flour with a pastry blender. Add melted ice cream and blend well. Refrigerate for 10 minutes.

Divide dough into two parts. Work with half the dough, leaving the remainder refrigerated. On a lightly floured sheet of wax paper, roll out dough to a rectangle 10-by-12 inches. Spread sparingly with preserves. Sprinkle with half the raisins and nuts.

Starting at the wide end, roll up as for a jelly roll. You may find it easier to start the roll with your fingers, then complete it by slowly lifting the edge of the wax paper nearest you. A few lifts and the dough has rolled itself. Complete this process with the remainder of the dough.

Cut into 1½-inch slices. Bake on ungreased cookie sheet at 350° until golden brown, about 35 minutes.

Elsie Sagerman's

CREAM CHEESE STRUDEL

¼ lb. cream cheese
¼ lb. butter
2 c. flour

Cream together cheese and butter, work in flour. Cover bowl and refrigerate overnight.

Divide dough in half. Roll out each half, very thin, on lightly floured wax paper. Spread with filling (below). Roll up tight (as for a jelly roll). Place on cooky sheet.

Bake at 375° for 25 minutes. Cut in ½-inch diagonal slices while still slightly warm.

SUGGESTED FILLINGS

1. Your favorite preserves (red raspberry is delicious, as is apricot).
2. Cinnamon-sugar mix with finely chopped nuts.

It depends upon the section of the country in which you live whether you call the ingredient in this recipe hoop cheese, farmer's cheese or dry cottage cheese, but wherever you are you'll enjoy Mrs. Harry (Lee) Greenberg's Cheese Dreams. Lee, who lives in Los Angeles, calls it hoop cheese. She says that this same recipe may be used in making knishes.

CHEESE DREAMS

½ pt. commercial sour cream
½ lb. softened butter
2½ c. flour
¼ tsp. salt
4 lb. hoop (dry cottage) cheese
4 eggs
4 Tbs. flour
12 Tbs. sugar
Juice of 1 lemon
Cinnamon to taste
Butter for dotting
½ c. cinnamon-sugar mix (½ c. sugar, 1 tsp. cinnamon)
½ c. cornflake crumbs

Blend sour cream and softened butter well. Stir flour and salt together and blend into sour cream-butter mixture. Cover with a cloth and refrigerate for several hours or overnight.

When ready to bake, combine cheese, eggs, 4 Tbs. flour, 12 Tbs. sugar, lemon juice and cinnamon.

Divide dough into 5 parts. Roll each part on a floured pastry board to a rectangle 6-by-17 inches. Place ⅕ of the filling down the center of the rectangle. Fold one side of the dough over the filling. Fold remaining side to overlap. This will make a roll about 2 inches wide and 17 inches long. Place the roll, seam side down, on a buttered cookie sheet. Place rolls 2 inches apart. Dot with butter and sprinkle with the cinnamon-sugar and crushed corn flakes, which have been combined.

Bake at 325° until golden brown, about 40 to 50 minutes. May be served with sour cream and strawberry jam.

"This recipe was developed as all our old recipes were," says Alice (Mrs. Nathan) Rosenberg of East Greenwich, Rhode Island. "One day, my aunt, my cousins, and I stood around my mother as she prepared Hamentaschen. We 'caught' the ingredients as she started to *gees ahrein*, and we measured them. We then went home and used these measurements. After several attempts and much improvising, we finally came up with The Recipe. Now we have happy and loving memories of our dear ones in their recipes for holiday goodies."

HAMENTASCHEN

3 c. flour
3 tsp. baking powder
¼ tsp. salt
½ c. sugar
¾ c. butter or shortening
3 eggs, well beaten
1 egg for brushing

Sift together flour, baking powder, salt and sugar. Cut in shortening. Add well beaten eggs and mix to a soft dough. On a floured board, roll out to ¼-inch thickness. Cut into 4- or 5-inch rounds. Place a teaspoon of filling in the center of each round Pinch edges together to form a triangle. Brush with beaten egg. Place on a well-greased baking sheet. Bake at 400° 12 to 15 minutes.

POPPY SEED FILLING

½ lb. poppy seed
¾ c. honey
½ c. sugar
1 orange, juice and grated rind
1 lemon, juice and grated rind
1 egg

Scald poppy seed. Drain well. Put through food chopper. Add remaining ingredients. Place in a saucepan. Bring to a boil. Boil 2 to 3 minutes. Cool before using.

PRUNE FILLING

1½ c. prunes, cooked and pitted
1½ c. raisins
1 orange, juice and grated rind
1 lemon, juice and grated rind
¾ c. sugar
1 tsp. cinnamon
½ c. chopped nuts

Chop prunes and raisins. Place in saucepan. Add remaining ingredients. Cook until slightly thickened. Cool before using.

Ann Bush's

CHEESE HAMENTASCHEN

1 cake yeast
½ c. lukewarm milk
3 c. sifted flour
2 Tbs. sugar
¼ tsp. salt
½ lb. butter
2 egg yolks
1 egg for brushing

Dissolve yeast in milk. Let stand in warm place 25 minutes. Sift together the sifted flour, sugar and salt. Work in butter.

Add 2 beaten egg yolks and yeast mixture. Knead dough. On a floured board, roll out dough to ¼-inch thickness. Cut in 4- or 5-inch rounds. Put a scant tablespoon of filling in the center of each round. Pinch edges together to form a triangle. Place on a greased cookie sheet. Brush tops with an egg which has been beaten with 1 or 2 Tbs. water.

Cover and let rise for 1 hour. Bake at 350° for about 18-20 minutes.

CHEESE FILLING

8 oz. cream cheese
1 egg yolk
¼ c. sugar
½ tsp. vanilla extract
1 Tbs. flour

Cream the cheese. Add remaining ingredients and beat until smooth and creamy.

My friend Bessie's Hamentaschen recipe follows:

HAMENTASCHEN

4 c. flour
2 cakes yeast
1 c. lukewarm milk
¼ lb. butter, melted
1 tsp. salt
1 heaping Tbs. shortening, melted
¾ c. plus 1 Tbs. sugar
3 eggs, well beaten
Milk for brushing tops

Put flour into mixing bowl. Make a well, into which crumble the yeast. Add milk. Do not stir. Cover and set in warm place until it starts to bubble. Add butter and shortening. Add salt, sugar and beaten eggs. Blend well. Cover and set in warm place to rise until double in bulk, about an hour. Punch down. Allow to rise again until double in bulk, about an hour. On floured board, knead lightly until dough is manageable. Roll out to ¼-inch thickness. Cut into 3-inch rounds. Place a teaspoon of filling in the center of each round. Bring three sides of the circles together at the centers to form triangles. Pinch the edges together to form a slight ridge. Place on a greased and lightly floured baking sheet. Brush tops with milk. Bake at 350° until well browned, about 15 to 18 minutes.

PRUNE FILLING

1 lb. prunes
1 c. raisins
½ c. finely chopped nuts
Grated rind of ½ orange
¼ c. sugar (or to taste)

Cook prunes until soft. Pit and chop fine. Pour boiling water over raisins. Let stand until soft. Drain raisins and chop. Add to prunes. Add nuts, orange rind, and sugar. Mix thoroughly.

CHEESE FILLING

12 oz. cottage cheese, sieved
2 eggs, well beaten
1 Tbs. cracker meal
½ tsp. cinnamon
⅓ c. sugar

Mix together thoroughly.

This Mandel Brodt is a favorite of Mrs. Philip (Minnie) Weinberger, who shares "Best Cook" honors in Charleston, South Carolina, with her friend Mrs. Manning Bernstein. Together, they have often provided mouth-watering treats for the congregation of historic Temple Beth Elohim.

MANDEL BRODT

¼ lb. butter
1 c. sugar
3 eggs
1 tsp. vanilla extract
1 tsp. lemon extract
1 tsp. baking powder
2¾ c. flour
1 c. sliced almonds

Cream together butter and sugar. Add eggs, one at a time, beating after each addition. Blend in flavorings. Mix baking powder into flour and add to creamed mixture. Fold in almonds.

Divide dough into 3 equal parts. With lightly floured hands, form each part into a roll 10 inches long, 1½ inches wide, and about 1 inch deep.* Place on a greased cookie sheet. Bake at 350° until firm to the touch, about 25 minutes.

Remove from oven. Cut diagonally into ¾-inch slices. Lay slices, cut side down, on cookie sheet. Sprinkle with sugar. Return to oven and toast to a golden brown, about 15 minutes.

*These rolls double in width when baked, so you must be the judge of the size Mandel Brodt that you want.

Dorothy Hyman of Silver Springs, Maryland, is noted for her Mandel Brodt. You'll love this crisp, not-too-sweet delicacy.

MANDEL BRODT

3 eggs
1 c. oil
1 c. sugar
1 tsp. vanilla extract
1 c. almonds, coarsely chopped
3 c. (or more) flour
Pinch of salt
2 tsp. baking powder
½ c. cinnamon-sugar mix (½ c. sugar, 1 tsp. cinnamon)

Beat eggs well. Add oil slowly, continuing to beat. Add sugar slowly, continuing to beat. Add vanilla. Fold in almonds.

Sift together 3 cups flour, salt and baking powder. Fold flour into egg mixture. Dough should come away from the sides of the bowl, but not be too dry. If necessary, add more flour.

Divide dough into 6 equal parts. Form each part into a strip 12 or 15 inches long and 2 inches wide. Place on a greased cookie sheet. Sprinkle with cinnamon-sugar mix. At 1-inch intervals, slice diagonally ¾ way through strip. Bake at 350° 30-40 minutes. Remove from oven. Complete the slicing.

Mrs. Nathaniel I. (Belle) Sandler of Providence, Rhode Island, provides us with this recipe for a different kind of Mandel Bread. It's untoasted.

MANDEL BREAD

¼ c. vegetable shortening
½ c. sugar
2 eggs, well beaten
Grated rind of ½ lemon
1⅔ c. sifted flour
1½ tsp. baking powder
1 tsp. vanilla extract
¼ c. chopped almonds
¼ c. white raisins

Blend together shortening, sugar and eggs. Beat well. Add grated lemon rind. Sift together flour and baking powder. Add to first mixture. Fold in vanilla, nuts and raisins. Fashion into two long, even strips. Place on greased cookie sheet. Bake at 350° for 25 minutes. Slice diagonally into 1-inch slices.

"When I served Periskes at our grandson's *Pidnya-ha-ben,* our guests were puzzled . . . they didn't know what it was," says Mrs. Ben Schlicht of Enigma, Georgia. "Once they tasted it, they pronounced it finger-lickin' good!"

PERISKES

FILLING

2½ lb. carrots, grated
3 c. sugar
¼ c. water
½ to 1 tsp. ground ginger*

Boil carrots, sugar and water, uncovered, until mixture holds its shape. Stir in ginger. Set aside while preparing dough.

DOUGH

2½ c. flour
2 Tbs. poppy seed
Pinch of salt
6 eggs, slightly beaten
¾ c. corn oil
1 pt. honey, for basting

Combine flour, poppy seed and salt in a mixing bowl. Make a depression in center into which pour eggs and oil. Combine and knead until dough holds its shape. This will make a soft dough. It may be necessary to add a little more flour.

On a lightly floured board, roll dough out thin to about ⅛ inch. Cut into 2-inch squares or circles. Place a small amount of filling in the center of each. Fold over into triangles or half-moons. Press edges together to seal.

Bake on greased baking tin at 400° until light brown, 10-12 minutes. Remove immediately to a large bowl. Cover with honey and baste several times while still hot. Remove to a buttered platter to dry.

*If you like ginger, so use more ginger. If you don't like it so much, use less, and if you can't stand ginger altogether so leave it out entire! After all, in your kitchen, you're the queen, so do it the way you like.

AUNT ANNIE KASDAN'S TAYGLECH

4 eggs
3 Tbs. oil
2½ c. flour
1 tsp. baking powder
1½ cups honey
¾ c. sugar
½ lb. pecan halves
1 Tbs. ground ginger (or more, to taste)
2 Tbs. bourbon or water

Beat together eggs and oil.

Sift together flour and baking powder. Add to egg mixture and knead in bowl until smooth. Pinch off pieces of dough and roll between the palms of your hands to form ropes ½ inch or less in diameter. Cut ropes into ½-inch pieces.

Bring honey and sugar to a rapid boil in a Dutch oven or any heavy, broad-bottomed pan with a tight cover. Drop dough into boiling honey a few pieces at a time, so the temperature will not fall below the boiling point. Cover and boil for 5 minutes. Remove from flame, stir and cover. Place in a 375° oven for 30-45 minutes, removing to stir at 15-minute intervals. At the end of 30 minutes, remove one piece. Test by breaking open with a fork. If it is not crisp, return to the oven for another 15-minute period. If crisp, stir in nuts and ginger. Remove from oven. Sprinkle with bourbon or cold water.

Turn out on a wet wooden board. Using a wet rolling pin, gently spread Tayglech to 1½-inch thickness. Dip hands in ice water and shape into a large square. When cool, cut into squares or diamond shapes of the desired size. Store in a tightly covered tin.

Mrs. Sidney (Carmen) Lipshutz of Louisville gives us an old family recipe with a new twist—you shouldn't have to lick the fingers.

AUNT IDA'S PARTY TAYGLECH*

4 c. sifted flour
3½ tsp. baking powder
6 Tbs. oil
6 eggs, slightly beaten
3 cups honey
2¼ c. water
2 c. sugar
4½ tsp. ground ginger
10 oz. pecan halves
¾ c. boiling water

Combine flour, baking powder, oil and eggs. Beat until well blended. Put dough on a floured pastry board and knead until smooth. Pinch off pieces of dough about the size of golf balls. Roll between the palms of your hands into strips about ½ inch thick. Cut strips into ½-inch pieces. Let stand while preparing syrup.

Let honey and water come to a boil in a large kettle. Stir constantly. (Do not use enamel or graniteware kettle.) Add sugar slowly. When syrup has returned to a full boil, drop the pieces of dough into the kettle, a few at a time. Cover and let boil until the dough is golden brown, about 18-20 minutes. Stir once or twice during this period. Stir in ginger and pecans. Add the boiling water. Cover the kettle and remove from the fire.

When the syrup no longer bubbles, turn the Tayglech out into a roaster or any large container. With a party pick, pierce through a pecan half and then through Tayglech.*

Place on a lightly oiled platter to cool. Continue the process until all the nuts and Tayglech have been speared.

*These toothpick Tayglech are a wonderful invention. Naturally, you want your guests to tell you that they were so good "you can lick the fingers from them," but who wants sticky-fingered guests?

Mrs. Herbert (Estelle) Fine of Cranston, Rhode Island, provides this recipe for tasty Tayglech.

QUICK TAYGLECH

3 eggs, beaten
1 Tbs. oil
¼ tsp. salt
¼ tsp. nutmeg
1¼ to 1½ c. flour
¾ c. (approx.) nuts, chopped
¾ c. (approx.) raisins, chopped
¾ cup honey
1½ c. sugar
½ c. water
Ground ginger

Combine eggs, oil, salt and nutmeg. Add enough flour to make a soft dough that will leave the sides of the bowl clean.

On a slightly floured board, roll or stretch dough very thin—almost as thin as for strudel.

Cut dough into small squares, about 1½ inches. Place some raisins and nuts in the center of each square. Seal dough around fruit.

In a large broad-bottomed saucepan (your grandmother used a copper pan), bring to a boil honey, sugar and water. Drop Tayglech into boiling syrup, a few at a time. Cover. Reduce heat. Simmer for 1 hour. After 15 minutes, stir gently. Stir again at the end of the hour.

Pour ¼ cup boiling water over Tayglech. Sprinkle with ginger.

With a slotted spoon, remove Tayglech to an oiled platter to cool. Store in a tightly covered tin.

❤ 20 ❤

Pesach Isn't Pesach Anymore

"If you ask me," Bessie started off . . . she always starts off that way, perhaps because no one ever asks her. I'm her best friend and even I don't ask her. Why should I? Would I ask for a tornado or a flood?

"If you ask me," said Bessie, "*Pesach* isn't *Pesach* anymore. It's Passover."

"Bessie," I said, "*Pesach* and Passover are the same thing. *Pesach* is Hebrew, Passover is English. It means when the angel of death 'passed over' the Israelites."

"What are you, a Sunday-school teacher?" said Bessie. "You think you'll teach me about Jewish holidays? If you ask me, I could teach you a thing or two. When I was a child, Passover was *Pesach*. What's more, it was a real *yom tov*. Now it's just a holiday."

"Bessie, *yom tov* and holiday . . ."

"I know, I know," said Bessie, "*yom tov* means holiday and holiday means *yom tov*, but still it isn't the same thing."

I could see that Bessie was working herself into a mood, so I tried to change the subject. "My son-in-law sent me a big box of Passover chocolates," I said. "Two pounds."

"You see," said Bessie, "that's exactly what I was talking about!"

"You never mentioned chocolates!"

"I was coming to that. Did you have chocolates for *Pesach* when you were a child? Never!"

"What do you mean, chocolates for *Pesach*?" I said. "I never had chocolates even *not* for *Pesach*. Who could afford them?"

"There you go with the hearts and flowers," said Bessie. "So you didn't have chocolates. You had penny candy, yes? But not for *Pesach*. You knew it was *Pesach* because for eight days you couldn't have candy. I think I spent the whole eight days just looking in the candy-store window."

"So?"

"So I knew it was *Pesach*! Nowadays you don't have to give up practically anything for *Pesach* except bread. You can have chocolates and even Coca-Colas. I'm waiting until they'll make ice cream '*Kosher le Pesach*.' Then I'm giving up completely."

"I don't understand what you're so worked up about, Bessie."

"I thought you were more intelligent," said Bessie. "I thought you would understand. If he doesn't give up anything, how can a child know what a happy *yom tov Pesach* is?"

"There's still the Seder, the ceremonial feast," I said, "when the story is retold of how the Israelites fled bondage in Egypt. And there's the matzoth, the unleavened bread they baked on their flight."

"Of course, there's the matzoth." Bessie started to laugh. She laughed until the tears came to her eyes. "Who can forget the matzoth," she said. "Remember the sandwiches we used to take to school?"

"I didn't take sandwiches," I said. "We lived across the street from the school."

"You didn't take sandwiches?" said Bessie. "So you missed all the fun. To my dying day I won't forget the chunks of yesterday's pot roast between two pieces of matzoth. I was the only Jewish girl in my class. I used to beg Mama not to give me a sandwich. I cried. I told her I'd rather starve. I used to say, 'Mama, everyone will look at me!' But Mama just said, 'Good, let them look, because if they will look they will ask what it is, and you'll tell them that this is the bread of affliction which your forefathers ate when they ran away from slavery. You can tell them this is freedom bread!'"

"So the children can say that now," I said.

Bessie looked at me and shook her head. "Where have you been all these years?" she asked. "Who takes matzoth sandwiches anymore? Now it's popovers! Of course, they're made from matzoth meal, but who will ask about popovers? A whole new industry has started up on how to make *Pesach* like every day. Somewhere women are making a living from dreaming up recipes for popovers, brownies and doughnuts made from matzoth meal! So at Seder, when the father asks, 'Wherefore is this night different from all other nights?' if the answer wasn't written down in the book, the child wouldn't know what to say. When I was a child, a Seder was a Seder! After the Seder was over, Mama would put out a bowl of oranges, one for each of us.

When did we ever eat an orange? On *Pesach*, or when we were sick, maybe we had an orange. If my grandson doesn't have his orange juice every day, my daughter-in-law thinks he's getting beriberi. I had an orange once a year only, and I still have all my own teeth . . . only one partial."

"Bessie," I said, "something is bothering you, and it isn't chocolates for *Pesach*."

Bessie was quiet for a second, which is a long time for Bessie. "You know," she said, "I think you're right. I got a letter this morning from the children. They can't come for *Pesach*. So when you came in, I was sitting and thinking. I was thinking, What's the fun of *Pesach* if you haven't got children in the house? Who will enjoy my *gefulte* fish and *knaidlech*? It doesn't pay to cook if you've got nobody in the house."

"They didn't invite you to visit them?"

"What do you mean?" Bessie was offended. "Naturally, they invited us."

"So why don't you go?"

"To tell you the truth I didn't think of it. We're so used to their coming here," said Bessie. "But it's hard for them to travel with young children."

"So you should go to them."

"Maybe it would be imposing," said Bessie. "It's not easy for a young girl to make *Pesach* with small children to take care of."

"So what's the matter with you? You don't know how to help out? The same things you make here, you'll make there."

"That's a wonderful idea," said Bessie. "Why didn't I think of it? I could bake them cakes and brownies, even popovers and doughnuts. Do me a favor," said Bessie. "Don't tell anyone I was talking so foolishly. *Pesach* is still *Pesach*, even if it is called Passover."

"The recipe for this Passover cake," says Marian Sachs, "came from an old friend of my mother. Her kitchen always smelled exquisite, but she was one of those cooks who never heard of measurements."

PASSOVER ALMOND-CARROT CAKE

1 c. finely ground almonds
1 c. sugar
8 eggs (4 whole eggs plus 4 yolks, reserve whites)
1 carrot, finely grated
1 lemon, juice and grated rind
½ c. matzoth cake meal

Combine almonds, sugar, 4 whole eggs and 4 egg yolks. Add grated carrot, juice and grated rind of lemon. Fold in cake meal. Stir until well blended. Beat 4 egg whites until they form soft peaks. Fold into first mixture. Bake in 9-inch tubed spring form which has been greased and lightly dusted with matzoth cake meal. Bake at 375° for 40 to 45 minutes. Invert to cool.

This recipe comes from Jean Siegel of Providence, Rhode Island. You'll love it!

PASSOVER APPLE SQUARES

1 c. sugar
½ tsp. salt
1 c. matzoth meal
3 eggs, separated
½ c. peanut oil
1 lemon, juice and grated rind
2 large apples, pared and sliced
Cinnamon-sugar mix

Combine sugar, salt and matzoth meal. Add egg yolks, oil and the juice and grated rind of lemon.

Fold in stiffly beaten egg whites.

Pour half this batter into a greased 8-by-8 inch pan. Cover batter with thinly sliced apples. Sprinkle with sugar and cinnamon mix. Cover with remaining batter.

Bake at 375° for 45 minutes. Cool. Cut into squares.

A busy woman is Marion (Mrs. James) Goldsmith of Providence, Rhode Island. Wife, mother (three teen-agers) and practicing psychiatric social worker, Marion still finds time for baking. Here's the family's favorite Passover dessert.

PASSOVER APRICOT WHIPPED PIE

MERINGUE SHELL

3 egg whites
¼ tsp. salt
¾ c. granulated sugar

Beat egg whites with salt until quite stiff. Gradually add sugar, continuing to beat until glossy.

Spread about ⅔ of this meringue over the bottom and sides of an 8- or 9-inch pie plate.

Drop remaining meringue in small rounds on a greased cookie sheet, pulling the meringues up into points. These small meringues will be used to top the pie.

Bake at 275° until light brown and crisp, about 1 hour. Cool on wire rack, away from drafts.

FILLING

1 lb. dried apricots
4 Tbs. sugar (or to taste)
Juice of ½ lemon
1 c. heavy cream
1 tsp. sugar

Cook apricots with sugar, lemon juice and just enough water to cover, about 1 pint. Cook until apricots are soft and water has been absorbed. Cool and mash.

Whip cream with 1 teaspoon sugar. When firm, blend in with cooled apricots. Fill shell. Decorate with small meringues. Refrigerate until ready to serve.

Mrs. W. L. (Shirley) Grossman, a schoolteacher and the mother of a teen-age son and daughter, says that baking is her favorite household pastime. Shirley lives in Buffalo, New York. Her recipe for Passover Brownies follows:

PASSOVER BROWNIES

2 Tbs. cocoa
2 Tbs. hot water
½ c. butter, melted
1 c. sugar
2 eggs, well beaten
½ tsp. vanilla extract
½ c. broken nuts
6 Tbs. matzoth cake meal
6 Tbs. potato starch

In a mixing bowl, dissolve cocoa in hot water. Add melted butter and sugar. Stir well. Add beaten eggs, vanilla and nuts. Fold in the cake meal which has been mixed with potato starch. Pour into a well-buttered 9-inch square cake pan. Bake at 350° for 20 minutes. Cool. Cut into squares.

This recipe comes from you know who. If you listen to her, it's the best cake in the world. Also, it's healthy, she claims, because the lemon and orange juice give you vitamins.

BESSIE'S PASSOVER CHIFFON CAKE

12 eggs, separated
2 c. sugar
½ orange, juice and grated rind
1 c. potato starch
1 lemon, juice and grated rind
Pinch of salt

In an electric mixer, beat egg yolks until thick. Slowly add sugar, continuing to beat. Add grated rinds and juice of lemon and orange. By hand, fold in potato starch. Add salt to egg whites and beat until very stiff. Fold into first mixture. Pour into a 10-inch ungreased tube pan. Bake at 375° until cake tests done, about 60-65 minutes. Invert to cool.

Mrs. David (Shirley) Bailen of Louisville provides the following recipe for a Passover treat:

PASSOVER CHEESE CAKE

½ lb. cream cheese
½ lb. creamed cottage cheese
⅔ c. sugar
2 Tbs. potato starch
5 large eggs, separated
1 tsp. vanilla

Cream cheeses together until smooth.

Mix together sugar and potato starch; add to cheeses while continuing to beat. Add egg yolks and vanilla. Beat until smooth. Beat egg whites until stiff and dry. Fold into the first mixture.

Pour into an 8-inch spring form which has been buttered and lightly dusted with potato starch. Bake at 350° for 45-50 minutes. Cool in the oven with door open. This cake will rise quite high and then sink. It may be topped with a fruit glaze.

The recipe for this light, fine-textured cake was contributed by Estelle Fine.

PASSOVER CHOCOLATE CAKE

8 eggs, separated
1½ c. sugar
1 orange, juice and grated rind
2 Tbs. cocoa
¼ c. Concord grape wine
¾ c. sifted matzoth cake meal

Beat egg yolks. Gradually add sugar, continuing to beat. Add rind and juice of orange, cocoa and wine. Fold in sifted cake meal. Fold in stiffly beaten egg whites. Bake in 10-inch tube pan at 350° for 50 minutes.

A Passover treat from Mrs. Harry Nussbaum follows:

CHOCOLATE APPLE TORTE

3 or 4 firm winter apples
Cinnamon-sugar mix
6 eggs, separated
1½ c. sugar
3 Tbs. cocoa
1 tsp. cinnamon
¾ tsp. ground cloves
¾ tsp. ground allspice
1 oz. sweet wine
6 tsp. (heaping) matzoth meal

Pare and quarter apples. Spread them on the bottom of a 9-inch spring form. Sprinkle lightly with cinnamon-sugar mix. Bake at 350° until just soft. Cool. Then cover the apples with the following mixture:

Beat egg yolks until thick. Gradually add sugar, continuing to beat. Add cocoa, spices, wine and matzoth meal.

Fold in stiffly beaten egg whites.

Bake at 350° for about 1 hour. Turn off heat. Let torte cool in oven with door open. Serve with whipped cream.

Tasty Passover Cookies from Betty Levine.

PASSOVER COOKIES*

1 c. oil
1 c. sugar
4 eggs
1 tsp. lemon juice
1¾ c. matzoth cake meal
1 Tbs. potato starch
½ c. finely chopped nuts

Combine oil, sugar and eggs. Beat until well blended. Add lemon juice.

Sift together cake meal and potato starch. Add to first mixture.

Drop from teaspoon onto greased cookie sheet. Sprinkle with nuts. Bake at 350° until golden brown, about 18-20 minutes.

*Once these cookies are mixed, try to get them into the oven very quickly. The texture changes if allowed to stand too long.

My friend Bessie says that this torte can be made with cracker meal to be served at any time, but why not make it with matzoth meal and keep it special just for *Pesach*?

DATE TORTE

8 eggs, separated
2 scant cups sugar
25 dates, cut up
½ c. chopped nuts
2 Tbs. cocoa
1 apple, grated
¼ tsp. ground cloves
½ tsp. ground allspice
1⅓c. matzoth meal
1 lemon, grated rind and juice
1 orange, grated rind and juice

Beat egg yolks until thick. Gradually add sugar, continuing to beat. Blend in remaining ingredients. Fold in stiffly beaten egg whites.

Bake in an ungreased 9-inch spring form which has been lined with wax paper. Bake at 350° for 50-60 minutes.

Bessie says that just because she doesn't like the idea of doughnuts for *Pesach* doesn't mean she can't make them.

PASSOVER DOUGHNUTS

⅔ c. water
⅓c. schmaltz*
1 Tbs. sugar
¼ tsp. salt
1 c. matzoth meal
3 eggs

Bring to a boil water, schmaltz, sugar and salt. Stir in matzoth meal. Cook for 1 minute. Remove from flame. Mix thoroughly. Cool slightly.

Beat in eggs, one at a time.

Grease hands. Roll dough into 2-inch balls. Place on greased cookie sheet. Dip index finger in water and press a hole in the center of each ball.

Bake at 375° for 50-60 minutes. Roll in granulated sugar.

*Rendered chicken fat.

21

The Last Chapter

Now that my book is finished, you're going to ask me, "So what's Jewish about it?" Did I tell you it was going to be a strictly Jewish bake book? No, I did not. What do you want from me? I've got in the book how to make strudel and *mandel brodt, taighlech* and *kichlech,* but I've got a lot of other delicacies, too. And didn't I tell you in the beginning that a lot of dishes you always thought were Jewish are very similar to other types of cooking?

I ate these delicious Jewish dishes at home, but I didn't learn to cook them there. My mother was a good cook but a very impatient teacher. Besides, she never used measurements. She belonged to what I call the *me nemt* school of cooking, the "you-take-a-little" school. You take a little flour, you take a little oil and an egg and you mix it until it "looks right" or "feels right."

Mama was not a good teacher, but I don't think that's why I didn't learn to cook when I was home. I think the real reason is that I was a first-generation American. My parents' background and culture differed from mine, so I felt that I had to prove my Americanism by discarding the old culture. What I didn't realize is that it is this amalgam of cultures that makes America unique.

Togetherness is a wonderful word, but it shouldn't mean sameness. Any mother will tell you that no two of her children are alike. Their very differences enrich family life. And it is these cultural differences that enrich our national life.

It's very difficult to adjust to a new culture or to a combination of cultures, although I must say the Jewish people have a genius for adapting themselves to new countries, and even for adopting regional loyalties, identification with a particular locale. I have in mind a certain shopkeeper in my community. One day when I was in his shop, he said to me, "Mrs. Kasdan, you're not ah Louisville girl, no?"

"No," I said, "I was born in Arkansas and grew up in Missouri. I'm not a Louisville girl."

"I taught you're not ah Louisville girl," said he. "You're not talkin' like we're talkin' here."

Although we adapt ourselves quickly, it isn't always easy. In a meeting of two cultures there is apt to be a clash. The cultural clash often takes place in the kitchen. This is true of any minority group. Imagine the first Italian family to move into a small community. There are children. The children go to school; they make friends. One day, the oldest son comes home from school and says, "Ma, I'd like to bring some of the fellows home for supper."

Mama is delighted. She sets about making a wonderful Italian dinner. Sonny should be happy, but he isn't.

"Gee whiz, Ma," he says, "why do you hafta make that stuff? The fellows'll laugh at me. Why don't you make Southern fried chicken?"

Mama doesn't listen to him. It's not that she doesn't want to, but she hasn't yet learned how to make fried chicken and biscuits. The boys don't laugh. They eat heartily. They have learned that strange foods can be good foods, and that strange people are not so strange when you get to know them. The way has been opened for a cultural exchange that will lead eventually to Sophia Loren and pizzerias.

Looking back on these cultural clashes from our vantage point, they seem very amusing. Remembering them makes us laugh, but sometimes I think there is only a thin line between laughter and tears. This is the essence of humor. This I learned in my search for Jewish recipes.

I had started out merely to learn more about Jewish cooking, so that a small part of my precious heritage might not be lost to me forever, but I learned more than Jewish cooking.

I learned that food is not just food; it has a certain symbolic character. To break bread with someone has always been considered a symbol of friendship. There is an intimacy about dining together that breaks down barriers and makes strangenesses disappear.

I learned, too, that Jewish cooking tells the story of my people. It's true that strudel is Hungarian, *schnecken* is Austrian, bourbon balls are American, but that is the story of the Jewish people. We have lived in every country on the globe. We have taken much from others, but we have added a flavor that is all our own and given them back something different and enriched.

This is our history. Let us take pride in it. To the bread of the world let us continue to add the sweetness of Jewish love, the salt of a Jewish tear, and the leavening of Jewish laughter.

• • Notes • •

• • Notes • •

• • Notes • •

• • Notes • •

• • Notes • •

• • Notes • •

Index

Almond Horns, 82
Apple Cake, 47
Apple Squares, Passover, 169
Apricot Bars, 34

Babka, 125
Bachelor Bars, 34
Banana Nut Loaf, 103
Bars, Apricot, 34
Bars, Bachelor, 34
Bars, Cherry Coconut, 36
Bar, Chocolate De-lite, 36
Bars, Coconut, 37
Bars, Date, 38
Bars, Dream, 39
Bars, Meringue, 40
Bars, Mother's Dream, 39
Bars, Pecan, 40
Basic Sweet Yeast Dough, 126
Blueberry Coffee Cake, 128
Bourbon Balls, 15
Bread, Banana Nut Loaf, 103
Bread, Challah, 72
Bread, Date Nut Loaf, 106
Brownies, 97
Brownies, Passover, 170
Cake, Apple, 47
Cake, Aunt Dora's Tomato Soup, 69
Cake, Carrot, 109-112
Cake, Chiffon for Shabbos, 48
Cake, Chocolate, 104
Cake, Chocolate Layer, 50
Cake, Chocolate Sponge, 104
Cake, Chocolate with Yeast, 105
Cake, Danish Gold, 51
Cake, Date, 52
Cake, Feather, 53
Cake, Fruit Cocktail, 54
Cake, Fruited Honey, 23
Cake, Ginger, 54
Cake, Grandmother's Black Coffee, 55
Cake, Hickory Nut, 55
Cake, Honey, 21-24
Cake, Honey in a Roaster, 24
Cake, Honey with Brandy, 22
Cake, Hot Milk, 107
Cake, Kentucky Pecan, 57
Cake, Lekach (Honey Cake), 21
Cake, Mama's Carrot, 111
Cake, Maple Nut, 58
Cake, Meringue Spice, 58
Cake, Mock Pound, 59
Cake, My Best Pound, 62

Cake, Orange, 59
Cake, Orange Delight, 60
Cake, Passover Almond-Carrot, 168
Cake, Passover Chiffon, 170
Cake, Passover Chocolate, 171
Cake, Pauline Cook's, 61
Cake, Pineapple Fluff, 62
Cake, Pound, 63
Cake, Prune, 64
Cake, Prunella, 64
Cake, Pumpkin, 65
Cake, Quick Chocolate, 106
Cake, Raisin, 66
Cake, Red Velvet, 67
Cake, Texas Pecan Pound, 68
Cake, Tomato Soup, 69
Cake, Whipped Cream, 69
Cake, White, 70
Carrot Cake, Mama's, 111
Challah, 72
Cheese Cake, 113-120
Cheese Cake, Chocolate Chip, 118
Cheese Cake, Cream with Walnut Crust, 115
Cheese Cake, Party, 120
Cheese Cake, Passover, 171
Cheese Dreams, 154
Cheese Hamentaschen, 156
Cheese Pie, Cream, No Crust, 119
Cheese Pie, Cream with Cointreau, 116
Cheese Torte, 118
Cherries, Chocolate, 16
Cherry Coconut Bars, 36
Cherry Thumb Prints, 82
Chiffon Cake for Shabbos, 48
Chocolate Apple Torte, 172
Chocolate Cake, 104
Chocolate Cake with Yeast, 105
Chocolate Cherries, 16
Chocolate Chip Cheese Cake, 118
Chocolate De-lite Bars, 36
Chocolate Fruit Torte, 49
Chocolate Layer Cake, 50
Chocolate Peanut Clusters, 97
Chocolate Rose Leaves, 16
Chocolate Sponge Cake, 104
Chocolate Thumb Prints, 83
Cinnamon Nut Crisps, 84
Coconut Bars, 37
Coffee Cake (*The Chattanooga Times*), 128
Coffee Cake, Babka,125
Coffee Cake, Basic Sweet Yeast Dough, 126
Coffee Cake, Becie's, 127
Coffee Cake, Blueberry, 128
Coffee Cake, Coffee-Break, 130
Coffee Cake, Cream Cheese, 132
Coffee Cake, Crumb-Filled, 132
Coffee Cake, Form, 134
Coffee Cake, French, 135
Coffee Cake, Mama Annie's, 136
Coffee Cake, Meringue, 137
Coffee Cake, Mother's Viennese Kugelhof, 140
Coffee Cake, Pull-Apart, 138
Coffee Cake, Sour Cream, 139
Coffee Cake, Streusel, 139
Coffee Cake, Supreme, 131
Coffee-Break Cake, 130

Cookies, Almond Horns, 82
Cookies, Brownies, 97
Cookies, Cherry Thumb Prints, 82
Cookies, Chocolate Peanut Clusters, 97
Cookies, Chocolate Thumb Prints, 83
Cookies, Cinnamon Nut Crisps, 84
Cookies, Cooky Rings, 98
Cookies, Delcas, 84
Cookies, Doughnuts, 98
Cookies, Eier Kichel, 76
Cookies, Eier Kichlech, 76
Cookies, French Pastry Crescents, 85
Cookies, Fruit Slices, 86
Cookies, German Sour Cream Twists, 86
Cookies, Hard-Boiled Egg, 87
Cookies, Hungarian Butter Wreaths, 88
Cookies, Kichel, 77
Cookies, Kipfel, 89
Cookies, Mandel Bread, 159
Cookies, Mandel Brodt, 158-59
Cookies, Party Tayglech, 162
Cookies, Passover, 172
Cookies, Periskes, 160
Cookies, Quick Tayglech, 163
Cookies, Ruggelach, 90
Cookies, Southern Pecan Tartlets, 91
Cookies, Sugar, 92
Cookies, Tayglech, 161
Cookies, Tiny Schnecken and Tartlets, 92
Cookies, Twist Craze-1964, 93
Cookies, Viennese Wafers, 94
Cooky Rings, 98
Cottage Cheese Strudel, 151
Cottage Cheese Sweet Rolls, 132
Cream Cheese Cake with Walnut Crust, 115
Cream Cheese Coffee Cake, 132
Cream Cheese Icing, 51
Cream Cheese Pie with Cointreau, 116
Cream Cheese Strudel, 154
Crumb-filled Coffee Cake, 132

Danish Gold Cake, 51
Date Bars, 38
Date Cake, 52
Date-Nut Loaf, 106
Date Torte for Passover, 173
Delcas, 84
Doughnuts, 98
Doughnuts, Passover,173
Dream Bars, 38-39

Eier Kichel, 76
Eier Kichlech, 75

Favorite Fruit Torte, 53
Feather Cake, 53
Form Coffee Cake, 134
French Coffee Cake, 135
French Pastry Crescents, 85
Frosted Grapes, 17
Fruit Cocktail Cake, 54
Fruit Slices, 86
Fruited Honey Cake, 23

German Sour Cream Twists, 87

Ginger Cake, 54
Grandmother's Black Coffee Cake, 55
Grapes, Frosted, 17

Hamentaschen, 156-58
Hamentaschen, Cheese, 156
Hard-Boiled Egg Cookies, 87
Hickory Nut Cake, 55
Honey Cake, 21-24
Honey Cake, Fruited, 23
Honey Cake in a Roaster, 24
Honey Cake with Brandy, 22
Hot Milk Cake, 107
Hungarian Butter Wreaths, 88

Ice Cream Strudel, 153
Icing, Cream Cheese, 51
Icing, Quick Mocha, 50
Icing, Sour Cream, 51

Kentucky Pecan Cake, 57
Kichel, 77
Kichel, Eier, 76
Kichlech, Eier, 75
Kipfel, 89

Lekach (Honey Cake), 21-24

Mandel Bread, 159
Mandel Brodt, 158-59
Maple Nut Cake, 58
Meringue Bars, 40
Meringue Coffee Cake, 137
Meringue Spice Cake, 58
Mock Pound Cake, 59
Mother's Dream Bars, 39
Mother's Viennese Kugelhof, 140
My Best Pound Cake, 62

No-Crust Cream Cheese Pie, 119

Orange Cake, 59
Orange Delight Cake, 60

Party Cheese Cake, 120
Passover Almond-Carrot Cake, 168
Passover Apple Squares, 169
Passover Apricot Whipped Pie, 169
Passover Brownies, 170
Passover Cheese Cake, 171
Passover Chiffon Cake, 170
Passover Chocolate Apple Torte, 172
Passover Chocolate Cake, 171
Passover Cookies, 172
Passover Doughnuts, 173
Pauline Cook's Cake, 61
Pecan Bars, 40
Periskes, 160
Pie, Passover Apricot Whipped, 169
Pin Wheel Rolls, 141
Pineapple Fluff Cake, 62
Pound Cake, 63-64
Pound Cake, Texas Pecan, 68
Prune Cake, 64
Prunella Cake, 65
Pull-Apart Coffee Cake, 138
Pumpkin Cake, 65

Quick Chocolate Cake, 106

Quick Mocha Icing, 50
Quick Tayglech, 163

Raisin Cake, 66
Red Velvet Cake, 67
Rose Leaves, Chocolate, 16
Royale Chocolate Torte, 66
Ruggelach (Yeast Horns), 90

Schnecken, 142
Schnecken and Tiny Tartlets, 92
Schnecken, Viennese, 143
Sour Cream Coffee Cake, 139
Sour Cream Icing, 51
Southern Pecan Tartlets, 91
Streusel Coffee Cake, 139
Strudel a la Sadie, 152
Strudel, Bessie's, 150
Strudel, Cheese Dreams, 154
Strudel, Cottage Cheese, 151
Strudel, Cream Cheese, 154
Strudel, Ice Cream, 153
Sugar Cookies, 92
Sweet Rolls, Cottage Cheese, 132
Sweet Rolls, Pinwheel, 141
Sweet Rolls, Schnecken, 142
Sweet Rolls, Viennese Schnecken, 143

Tartlets, and Tiny Schnecken, 92
Tartlets, Southern Pecan, 91
Tayglech, Aunt Annie Kasdan's, 161
Tayglech, Aunt Ida's Party, 162
Tayglech, Quick, 163
Texas Pecan Pound Cake, 68
Thumb Prints, Cherry, 82
Thumb Prints, Chocolate, 83
Tiny Schnecken and Tartlets, 92
Torte, Cheese, 118
Torte, Chocolate Apple for Passover, 172
Torte, Chocolate Fruit, 49
Torte, Date, for Passover, 173
Torte, Favorite Fruit, 53
Torte, Royale Chocolate, 66
Twist Craze-1964, 93

Viennese Schnecken, 143
Viennese Wafers, 94

Wafers, Viennese, 94
Whipped Cream Cake, 69
White Cake, 70

Yeast Horns (Ruggelach), 90

The wonderful cooks who gave me the recipes

Alper, Edith
Alper, Millie
Altman, Naomi

Bailen, Shirley
Berkovitz, Sali
Bernstein, Mildred
Blate, Mrs. Maurice
Blieden, Anna Leah
Bordorf, Hilda
Brooklyn, Carol
Bush, Ann

Charlip, Naomi
Claugus, Suzanne
Cohen, Diane
Cohen, Elizabeth
Cohen, Mrs. Leslie S.
Cohen, Mrs. K.
Conn, Irene

Davis, Mrs. Milton C.

Elkin, Lee

Fine, Estelle

Gertz, Minnie
Goldsmith, Marion
Goldstein, Rose
Greenburg, Lee
Grossman, Shirley

Halpern, Judith
Hoffman, Maxine
Hollander, Mrs. H.L.
Hornung, Mary
Hyman, Dorothy
Hyman, Sylvia

Jacobs, Phyllis

Kaplan, Lucille
Kasdan, Aunt Annie
Kasdan, Reva
Keil, Rose
Kline, Mrs. Maurice
Kohn, Frenchy
Konigsberg, June

Lapp, Elise
Leventhal, Sara
Levine, Betty
Lipshutz, Carmen

Marks, Celia
Mayer, Mariam
Michel, Margaret
Myers, Minna

Nussbaum, Rhoda

Perlman, Edith
Potash, Becie

Reinglass, Mrs. Samuel
Rosenberg, Alice
Rosenblatt, Dinah R.
Rosenfield, Lois
Rubel, Mrs. Henry

Sachs, Marian
Sagerman, Annette
Sagerman, David
Sagerman, Elsie
Sandler, Belle
Saul, Helen
Settle, Sarah
Shaw, Edna
Siegel, Jean
Silverman, Sarah
Simon, Selma Jean
Siskin, Minnie
Smith, Bella
Spain, Goldye
Starr, Irene
Stern, Mrs. Joseph

Thorpe, Shirley
Trivers, Sarah

Waldman, Ruthie Faye
Webster, Lucille
Weinberger, Minnie
Weisberg, Marian
White, Lillian

Zane, Mrs. Michael